Inspiring Creative Supervision

of related interest

Creative Supervision
The Use of Expressive Arts Methods in Supervision and Self-Supervision
Mooli Lahad
ISBN 978 1 85302 828 1

Inspiring Creative Supervision

Caroline Schuck and Jane Wood

Illustrated by Jane Wood

Jessica Kingsley *Publishers*
London and Philadelphia

First published in 2011
by Jessica Kingsley Publishers
116 Pentonville Road
London N1 9JB, UK
and
400 Market Street, Suite 400
Philadelphia, PA 19106, USA

www.jkp.com

Library of Congress Cataloguing in Publication Data
Schuck, Caroline.
  Inspiring creative supervision / Caroline Schuck and Jane Wood ; illustrated by Jane Wood.
    p. cm.
  Includes bibliographical references and index.
  ISBN 978-1-84905-079-1 (alk. paper)
  1. Group facilitation. 2. Supervision. 3. Workshops (Adult education) I. Wood, Jane, 1954- II. Title.
  HM751.S38 2011
  658.3'02--dc22
                          2010032855

British Library Cataloguing in Publication Data
A CIP catalogue record for this book is available from the British Library

ISBN 978 1 84905 079 1

Printed and bound in the UK

'Tell me, and I will forget. Show me, and I may remember. Involve me, and I will understand.' (Confucius c.450 BC)

Disclaimer

Every effort has been made to trace copyright holders and to obtain their permission for the use of copyright material. The authors and the publisher apologize for any omissions and would be grateful if notified of any acknowledgements that should be incorporated in future reprints or editions of this book.

Contents

List of Boxes and Figures

Boxes

Figures

About the Authors

Caroline Schuck is a qualified supervisor and homeopath with a background in humanistic psychotherapy. She teaches supervision skills and reflective practice at the University of Westminster, works one to one, runs groups and co-facilitates supervision skills workshops for the London Deanery.

Jane Wood is a qualified supervisor, teacher and homeopath, working in universities and colleges in London and Japan. She teaches supervision skills and runs workshops, as well as supervising groups and individuals internationally. She is a self taught artist.

Acknowledgements

Caroline would like to thank all her students, workshop participants, supervisees and colleagues who over the years have helped her deepen her understanding of the supervisory process. She would like to acknowledge the influence of Spectrum, Revision, the Tavistock, the London Deanery and the University of Westminster. She is indebted to her family for their unfailing love and support. She would like to thank Jane for making this creative journey with her.

Jane offers thanks and gratitude to everyone who has taught her so much over the years. Her loving appreciation goes to her students, supervisees and workshop participants in London and Japan, and her colleagues around the world. Her love and gratitude are for her family for their support and technical help. Her thanks go to Caroline for the many years of having fun, while working together.

Jane and Caroline would like to give special thanks to all those who allowed us to share their cases in this book.

Introduction

We met by chance at a supervisor's refreshment day and realized that we worked in similar ways. We started running workshops together, and in preparing for these we challenged each other to become more facilitative and less prescriptive, more creative and less bound by theory. We supervised each other, developing new techniques and sometimes dissolving into fits of laughter as we pushed our own boundaries and those of supervision itself. Over the many years that we have used creative supervision, we have watched numerous supervisees make great leaps in understanding, and we have felt humbled by the process. The most minimal of interventions can produce the maximum result. We hope, that in reading this book, you can share our enthusiasm and inspiration as you travel your own creative path.

Inspiring Creative Supervision provides you with a journey of exploration, using many different techniques and materials as well as the rich experience of the imagination and the senses. It encourages you to go beyond the formal demands of your role, and feel inspired by creativity, spontaneity and experiential work. At the same time, it is a practical reference book that can be used by you as a resource whether you are a teacher, supervisor, healthcare worker, therapist, mentor, coach or work in human resources.

We have worked as teachers, supervisors and facilitators of workshops, both together and individually, and it is our experience that creative methods of facilitation enhance learning. Over the years we have collected together a portfolio of techniques and resources that we have found consistently effective. Some of these originated in different fields; others we have extended and developed, and a few we have designed from the beginning. We have tried and tested all of them within a supervisory or teaching framework.

Much has been written, mainly in psychotherapeutic literature, about the role of the supervisor. The definitions all stress different aspects of supervision. Some look at the alliance, some focus on educational goals; others talk of the welfare of the client or the professional development of the supervisee. Most concentrate on the tasks of the session. Many authors agree that what happens is that, through the process of working together, new perspectives are opened up for the supervisee.

We see supervision as a collaboration in which two professionals agree to work together, focusing on the personal and professional development of one of them. The supervisory process is in itself a creative process because it involves a deep and multi-faceted reflective engagement by the supervisee that is triggered by apt and timely questioning by the supervisor.

In *Inspiring Creative Supervision* we offer you the possibility of further enhancing the supervisory experience by extending creativity beyond the bounds of everyday language. We have found that creativity has the same beneficial effect on adults as play has for children, helping them to develop and learn.

There are two aspects of creative supervision: the first one is the techniques used by the supervisor, and the second is the resources or materials that can be utilized. Examples of resources are puppets, toys, bricks, paper, coloured pens, stones, toy money and pictures. The skills and techniques include self-reflection, contracting, awareness of non-verbal communication, managing groups, facilitating a visualization, use of narrative skills and ritual. These two aspects are balanced between the structure necessary for safety and confidentiality, and the freedom and enthusiasm that creativity and play can bring.

Inspiring Creative Supervision can either be read from cover to cover or can be used as a reference book. We interweave chapters on skills and techniques with practical information on resources and how to use them. Because of the broad readership of this book we have had to make choices in the language that we use. In order to have some consistency we have generally used the terms 'supervisor' or 'facilitator' to describe the teacher, supervisor, facilitator, mentor or coach and 'supervisee' or 'storyteller' to describe the student, supervisee or group participant. Generally we use the word 'story' to describe the individual issue, problem or dilemma that the supervisee wishes to work on.

As we have worked with different groups and individuals over the years, we have developed and changed our techniques. Creativity would be lost if everything remained static and fixed. We have been fascinated by the endless possibilities of creative supervision and encourage you to use this book as a springboard for your own creativity and to take the ideas further.

Chapter 1

Introducing Creative Supervision

Supervision is a collaborative process in which the supervisor works with the supervisee to explore their work reflectively. The role of the supervisor is often viewed as a mix of educative, mentoring, holding the ethical position and ensuring the safety of the supervisee and of the supervisee's client. Fundamental to the relationship is good rapport and a working alliance.

Supervision methods have traditionally employed questioning in order to trigger reflective thinking. Both the supervisor and the supervisee are influenced by the role models that they have experienced, the systems they adhere to and the literature they have read. This affects how they work together, and for both of them the easiest way of working will be the one they know. However, working within safe and familiar boundaries can limit their learning. Exploring new methodologies and experiencing different ways of working together may at first feel unsafe for both the supervisor and supervisee, but there is much to be gained from it.

We start with giving you some background in relation to the theory of learning and teaching, and its relationship to facilitative teaching and facilitative supervision. This underpins the exercises that you will find later on in the book, and provides a link with the rationale for using them. We see a similarity between facilitative teaching and facilitative supervision, and therefore the techniques used in this book can be used in either setting.

Teaching and supervision both encourage the student or supervisee to take an active part in their own learning, and as such both are student centred. Leading on from this discussion of the facilitation of learning, we introduce our seven stages for working effectively and safely with creative supervision.

Learning styles

The two hemispheres of the brain are seen as being responsible for different functions. Most people have a dominant side of their brain that determines how they see the world. The left brain is considered to deal with rational thought, logic, linear, analytical and sequential thinking, calculating and mathematics. People who have a left-sided dominance tend to look at the details and then put them together to make a whole. The right brain processes emotion, feeling, intuition, creativity and emotional literacy within a group or society. People who process more readily in this mode take in information by looking at the whole picture and then the details. Western culture sometimes places a higher priority on rational thought and left-brained thinking, downplaying the importance of intuition and right-brained creativity. This may also be true of supervision, which has been traditionally engaged in through analysis and left-brained thinking.

For learning to be most effective, we suggest working with both sides of the brain, although probably not in equal proportion. The percentage of one side to the other will be influenced by a person's preferred and historical learning styles. The historical learning style is how the person was expected to learn at school, and it might (or might not) match the preferred learning style, or perhaps overlay it.

Several different preferred learning styles have been identified by educational theorists, although these vary according to sources. For example, there are people who are very intellectual, and enjoy fact finding and thinking through their work. Lectures and research might suit them. Others need experiential work, and get the most out of practice sessions and role-play. Other people learn through their senses; some are visual and will want to see pictures and diagrams, or notes written on a board; some are aural and like to listen to lectures, or to music while they work; others are tactile and need to touch something, taking notes or doodling while they listen. Others are verbal, need to talk through their work in order to understand it and work best in a team.

As a teacher or a supervisor, it can be useful to understand what kind of learners your students or supervisees are. If you work in a way that is accessible to them, they will feel comfortable working with you. At other times it is useful to challenge them outside their preferred learning style. This can create discomfort so it needs to be negotiated, but often it opens up new possibilities.

Teaching styles

Teaching and learning are two different things. There are many different ways of teaching, but we can simplify it by saying that teaching can be done from either side of the brain. As Knowles (1973) suggests in *The Adult Learner: A Neglected Species*, the traditional way of teaching (pedagogy) has the teacher in total control of the material and delivery:

> Pedagogy literally means the art and science of teaching children. The pedagogical model of education is a set of beliefs – indeed, as viewed by many traditional teachers, as an ideology – based on assumptions about teaching and learning that evolved in the seventh and twelfth centuries in the monastic and cathedral schools in Europe out of their experience in teaching basic skills to young boys...
>
> The pedagogical model assigns to the teacher full responsibility to make all decisions about what will be learned, how it will be learned, when it will be learned, and if it has been learned. It is teacher-directed education, and leaving the learner only the submissive role of following a teacher's instructions. (p.52)

Knowles (1973) goes on to propose that although this might be appropriate for small children – or for anyone starting an entirely new subject – as the child matures through adolescence to adulthood it becomes less and less appropriate:

> As individuals mature, their *need* and *capacity* to be self directing, to utilise their experience in learning, to identify their own readiness to learn, and to organise their learning around life problems, increases steadily from infancy to pre-adolescence, and then increases rapidly during adolescence. (p.53)

Andragogy or self-directed learning allows the student to be an active participant in their own learning. The teacher takes on the role of facilitator in this process and does the absolute minimum of directing or lecturing. The same happens in supervision when the supervisor chooses to facilitate rather than instruct.

Adult learners are on the whole at their most comfortable working within the andragogical model. While children learn whatever is presented to them in a teaching context, adults need personal motivation. Generally they have developed a very strong sense of self that needs to be respected. As adults, they have a much wider and broader life experience than when they were children. Through perceiving their gaps in knowledge, perhaps in relation to real-life situations, they will want to study to further their knowledge or learn new skills for dealing with problems. Professionals are generally motivated by a curiosity for learning and a need to develop in order to further their understanding and in turn their careers. Knowles (1973) again:

> Adults have a self-concept of being responsible for their own decisions, for their own lives. Once they have arrived at that self-concept they develop a deep psychological need to be seen by others and treated by others as being capable of self-direction. They resent and resist situations in which they feel others are imposing their wills on them. (p.57)

Therefore, if you are working with adults, as clients, students or supervisees, you will need to negotiate with them in order to motivate them. If you are interested in including creative supervision in your work, then advertise it clearly and explain it carefully when starting with new students or supervisees. If someone's mode of thinking is very left-brained and intellectual, they will be naturally resistant to creative work, and maybe it just does not suit them. However, were they to be willing, creative work could open up new possibilities for them, and may give them new insights.

As teachers, supervisors and workshop facilitators for over 20 years, we encourage as much self-directed learning and creative work as possible. It is our experience that working this way is dynamic and powerful, creating major shifts in understanding. Creative or experiential work cannot take over entirely, and may have to be interwoven with more directive or informative interventions at times. There are occasions when information needs to be shared and the teacher, facilitator or supervisor needs to be prescriptive, but these are pedagogic styles and we suggest they are kept to a minimum.

When supervisory relationships fail, it is often because of a lack of a clear working agreement. Taking time to negotiate carefully at the beginning of the relationship, and discussing the expectations of both parties, pays dividends. This gives an opportunity to clarify working styles and create an alliance.

Intervention styles

The work of Heron (1990) is widely used to understand the practitioner-client relationship and can also be used to understand the supervisor-supervisee or tutor-student relationship. As he says in *Helping the Client: A Creative Practical Guide*:

> Between practitioner and client there is a mutually agreed voluntary contract implicit in the relationship: the client chooses the practitioner and the service, and the practitioner chooses to accept the client. There is a formal differentiation of roles between them. And there will usually be a fairly clear understanding between them as to what the practitioner's remit is. (p.2)

Heron's six category interventions can be seen to link into the many different learning styles and the two teaching styles. The first three interventions are authoritative, where a supervisor or facilitator takes a more dominant or assertive role. These can be compared to pedagogy. First, there is the *prescriptive* intervention, where the supervisor is directive, explicitly guiding the work of the supervisee, in the manner of an expert; second, the *informative* one, where instruction is given or knowledge and information are shared; and, lastly, the *confrontative* intervention, where challenges are made in order to raise the supervisee's awareness.

The second three are facilitative interventions, where supervisors encourage supervisees to think for themselves and become more autonomous. These can be compared to andragogy. The *cathartic* intervention aims to release tension; the *catalytic* encourages self-reflection and self-directed problem solving; and the *supportive* approves, confirms and validates.

When a teacher, facilitator or supervisor is new to the work, the tendency might be to go towards the three authoritative intervention styles, because these will most likely fit in with the supervisor's own historical style of pedagogy. We suggest that you observe which mode of teaching and supervision you are using, and then challenge yourself to use a wider range of intervention styles. If you can be flexible in the way that you facilitate, your students or supervisees will parallel this and expand their learning styles.

We have found that the facilitative interventions are greatly enhanced by the use of creative supervision techniques. When we refer to creativity, we mean the ability to play and explore freely, like you did when you were a child. This is a universal ability, unrelated to age or artistic talent. In our experience, using play and creativity deepens the supervisee's understanding.

Power in the therapeutic relationship

As a supervisor or teacher working with adult learners, we recommend that you pay attention to the power dynamics implicit in your relationship. As the facilitator, you probably have more knowledge and experience in certain areas than your students or supervisees. Unconsciously, you may be viewed by them as an authority figure or an expert with all the answers. Alternatively, you may assume these roles for yourself. Taking on this stance can come from copying your role models or it may have evolved out of your own personal needs. Assuming power and expertise, or having it forced upon you, are both unhelpful for the relationship. Teachers or supervisors who are put on a pedestal may feel overawed by the responsibility, or guilty that they cannot deliver. They could become bullies or persecutors if they start to believe they are superior. The supervisees or students can feel disempowered, weak or helpless, and this prevents them from thinking for themselves. We suggest that it is beneficial for both if the relationship is kept on an equal adult-to-adult basis, with the supervisor or teacher acting as a facilitator.

Creative supervision is spontaneous, playful and experiential. Success in using it comes from ensuring that clear guidelines are given on how it is done. Supervisees needs to understand what is expected of them, and boundaries should be in place to create safety and security. Through our years of working this way, we have identified seven steps to the process (see Box 1.1). In the rest of this chapter, we write about the supervisor and the supervisee, but the same steps can equally apply to working as a teacher, coach, mentor, or in any therapeutic relationship.

Box 1.1 The seven stages of creative supervision

1. Making a clear contract with the supervisee or group.

2. Providing the resources and arranging the room.

3. Waiting in silence while people are working.

4. Giving fair, owned and balanced feedback on what is observed.

5. Engaging the supervisees in dialogue, discussion, critical thinking and action plan.

6. Encouraging them to write notes in their journals.

7. Ensuring that they come out of role.

---

1. MAKING A CLEAR CONTRACT OR WORKING AGREEMENT

Any one-to-one relationship, or group that meets regularly for teaching or supervision purposes, needs a long-term contract that sets down mutually agreed ground rules. Ideally this would include practicalities such as time, payment, frequency and location of meetings. It is also useful to encourage a group to consider their individual and group values and to add these to the contract. These might include confidentiality, respect and active listening skills. It is helpful to have a discussion about different ways of working and including the use of creative techniques.

When Caroline takes on new supervisees, she always asks them what their expectations are of the supervisory relationship. She also asks about their history of supervisory relationships. She tells them clearly what she can and cannot provide as a supervisor, and gives some details of how she works. She has a written contract, which is then tailor-made to each individual client. There are some aspects that are non-negotiable, such as fees and the need for notice of ending the relationship, but how they work together is co-created with each individual supervisee.

It is our experience that, when adult students or supervisees are launched into a new piece of work without fully understanding what is expected from them, they can react in a number of different ways such as becoming upset, irritable, resistant or simply spaced out. Adult learners respond best when feeling that they are in control of their learning, and, for this to happen, they need to plan and negotiate together with their tutor or supervisor. Doing this increases their sense of self and personal integrity as an adult. Without it, they can feel disempowered, which in turn makes them emotional or resistant and disrupts their ability to learn and explore. Knowles (1973) maintains that:

> a cardinal principle of andragogy (and, in fact of humanistic and adult education theory) is that the mechanism must be provided for involving all the parties concerned in the educational enterprise in its planning. One of the basic findings of applied behavioural science research is that people tend to feel committed to a decision or activity in direct proportion to their participation in or influence on its planning and decision-making. (p.123)

Even if there is a general agreement to work creatively, supervisees can be resistant when a new technique is suggested. They can relax when the methodology is familiar and may become anxious and fearful when offered something new. New ways of working can raise old anxieties about being exposed in public or made to feel deficient in some way. Added to this, supervisees can feel vulnerable, because they are bringing to supervision issues with which they need help. They might desire help in the spirit of a collegial relationship, but at the same time they may fear or fantasize that the supervisor will metamorphose into a teacher, judge, inquisitor or scolding parent.

All these fantasies and anxieties can be allayed by discussing the supervisees' previous experiences and creating a clear working agreement. As the supervisor, you might propose a particular technique to deal with a certain issue. You should explain what this would entail, and reassure the supervisee that it is an opportunity to play and explore without being judged. If the supervisee is still resistant, then you can negotiate to change, reduce or scrap the current suggestion. The key is in the negotiation. Nothing is to be gained by a prescriptive insistence on working in a way that appeals to the facilitator but frightens the supervisee.

CASE STUDY

When we run a workshop together, Caroline uses an opening exercise that both helps the participants let go of the stresses of their journey and encourages group formation. She begins with a mini-contract, using words to this effect:

I would like to do a relaxing opening exercise with you all. This is a simple session, where we all stand in a circle and I will guide you through a short visualization, during which you will be asked to touch your face. It's quite fun, and most people find it refreshing.

I hope this is okay with you? (She checks that everyone is okay with this.)

Please stand in a circle, make yourselves comfortable and, if you would like to take your shoes off, please do so. Close your eyes, make a fist with your hands and slowly start to massage your face starting with your forehead. Make circular movements with your fist, then work round your eyes; imagine you are rubbing the journey away. Now move down through your cheek bones and behind your ears; then move down your neck, making sure that you draw all the anxieties and difficulties in getting here into your fists. When they are all gathered together, take a deep breath in and, when I say so, fling your hands and arms out wide and give a shout as you open your eyes.

This is a gentle warm-up exercise that sets the tone of the work that is to come, and helps to bond the group. The mini-contract that precedes the exercise allows everyone to relax because they understand what will be expected of them. Using a mini-contract to introduce the warm-up reassures everyone about the security of the entire day. Notice that Caroline checked that everyone was willing to participate.

By doing this, she acknowledged that not everything will work for everyone. We have not had anyone who would not try this out, but should this be the case it would be fine to let them sit out and join in when they are ready.

2. ASSEMBLING RESOURCES AND ARRANGING THE ROOM

Once you have negotiated and agreed how to work, we suggest you get furniture, props and resources in place before starting. Preferably, you will have some resources with you, but you may not. You might need to have a quick look around the room, to collect suitable resources or props; or you may need to check that there is a good supply of paper and pens.

Leave yourself open to the possibility that you may not have everything that you need with you. Sometimes it is better to work spontaneously, using whatever resources are to hand. This models creative thinking for the supervisee, and adds an element of playfulness. An example of this was when Caroline was at a workshop and the facilitator needed a ball for the group to throw to each other. The exercise involved calling out their own name and the other person's name as they threw the ball. This was a way of learning each other's names. As there was no ball to hand, the group looked at how they could make a ball from what they had around them. A beautiful ball was made from a scarf tied into a knot. This group preparation for the warm-up activity helped to form the group as well as stimulate creativity. A different group might have come up with another, equally creative solution, such as screwing up paper or rolling a pair of socks into a ball.

Arranging the room to suit the work makes a remarkable difference to the feel or atmosphere of the session. It is like setting a stage. For example, if you are working one-to-one or in a group with picture postcards, you need to have enough space to spread the cards out on a large table or on the floor (see Chapter 6). A lack of suitable space to do the work can make everyone feel physically awkward or uncomfortable, and this in turn can cause resistance.

Sometimes group work needs to have a very specific arrangement of chairs. For example, the facilitator might want to sit opposite the case giver, with three or four observers either side. Would this be more comfortable as a rectangle, or a circle? In some sessions, you might want to use an empty chair to represent an absent person or thing. Where should the empty chair be placed in relationship to the supervisee? If you're arranging for the group to work in triads, be mindful that the dynamic changes in relation to how they sit. There will be a difference if they sit as a perfect triangle, or as a twosome, with the third at an unobtrusive distance.

We suggest that you take a couple of minutes before you start teaching or supervising to tune into your intuitive awareness of the atmosphere of the room. Does it feel comfortable? What can you do to improve it, considering that it might not be your room and there might be limited time? Usually a large bright window is a bonus to any room, but, if key speakers sit with their back to the light, the rest of the people in the room cannot see their face, and lose half of the presentation.

Often a quick rearrangement of furniture can make a tense, formal space into a friendly, relaxed working environment. Check that the room temperature, lighting and fresh air suits everyone, and respond to their needs.

3. WAITING IN SILENCE WHILE PEOPLE ARE WORKING

Most of the techniques presented in this book depend upon the supervisee or group accessing their hidden processes. They need to go into a quiet, intuitive or creative state that can sometimes be almost trancelike. Some people talk to themselves quietly under their breath while they are doing this, but on no account should you reply to them or question them. Talking to them, requiring an answer, demands that they think and, as soon as they activate the thinking brain, they lose touch with the intuitive state.

It is as if we cannot access both the thinking brain and the intuitive brain at the same time. Two examples of this come to mind. A woman who is in childbirth needs to go into a primitive, trancelike state, in order to go with the flow and enable her body to give birth. She does not notice the outside world, and makes little animal noises. As soon as she is asked to think – for instance, if the doctor has asked her if she needs medication, or the ambulance has arrived to take her to hospital – the birth process can often stop. Another example is young children who fall over and hurt themselves, and express their grief and anger with screams and tears. If you ask the child a question, and get them to focus their thinking mind, the tears and pain are forgotten. It doesn't matter if the question is about treats such as ice cream or the park, or a more practical question about where a certain toy was left.

It is quite clear when supervisees have finished the piece of creative work and are ready to talk. Their body language changes, and they sit back, relax or sigh. They look away from their creative work and around the room, or they meet the eyes of the supervisor.

4. FEEDING BACK YOUR OBSERVATIONS

We see feedback as the visual and/or verbal reply that is given after supervisees have presented information or done a piece of work. It includes both words and body language. The best feedback has integrity of intention, respect, authenticity and honesty. It demonstrates your interest in the supervisees and your intention to help them develop. The skill lies in giving this in a form and manner that allows the supervisees to accept it and make use of it.

Hawkins and Shohet (1989), in discussing the complexities of feedback in *Supervision in the Helping Professions: An Individual, Group and Organizational Approach*, say that:

> The process of telling another individual how they are experienced is known as feedback. Giving and receiving feedback is fraught with difficulty and anxiety because negative feedback restimulates memories of being rebuked as a child and positive feedback goes against injunctions not to have 'a big head'. Certainly most people give or experience feedback only when something is amiss. The feelings surrounding feedback often lead to it being badly given, so fears of it are often reinforced. There are a few simple rules for giving and receiving feedback that help it to be a useful transaction which can lead to change. (p.83)

Hawkins and Shohet recommend using a clear structure for which they use a mnemonic: CORBS: Clear, Owned, Regular, Balanced and Specific.

- *Clear*: In order to be clear, keep the feedback simple and short. The more you say, the more likely you are to complicate things.

- *Owned*: Keep your words personal. When you take ownership of the feedback, you're saying, 'This is my point of view. I notice, from my perspective, and someone else might say differently.' This distinguishes it from universal truths or fact.

- *Regular*: This applies to the ongoing relationship with the supervisee, where you should give feedback almost routinely in small, bite-sized portions, and not all at once.

- *Balanced*: Supervisees will find feedback more acceptable if it is given on both their strengths and their weaknesses. A good way of doing this is to sandwich the negative feedback between two positive comments.

- *Specific*: Avoid generalizations, be direct and say what you mean.

Most of the feedback in creative supervision is a tentative offering back of what has been observed. The supervisees re-create their original experience, through words, role-play, mime, toys, objects or a drawing. The supervisor or other group members give feedback on what they have observed. Feedback should begin as a simple observation, and may progress to an owned personal conclusion. Useful words that demonstrate ownership might be: 'I wonder if; I'm curious about; I'm interested in; can I make an observation? my feeling is; from where I am sitting I notice'.

CASE STUDY

Jane was supervising a group, and she asked the participants to represent their work using animals and figurines. She suggested that they used three or four different toy figures to represent different aspects of their work. One group member chose a wizard holding fire in his hand, a butterfly, a dolphin and a lion. The figures were placed closely together and were all going in the same direction. Jane suggested that this group member listened to feedback from everyone else, before sharing her thoughts on what she had done.

The group members variously observed that the figures were all moving in the same direction, and were acting as a sort of team, or unit. They were interested in the butterfly, which was of a completely different scale to the other characters. Jane observed:

> From where I am sitting, the group of figures seem quite purposeful, moving in the same direction, and I can imagine that they are helping each other. I agree with the others that the figures look like a sort of team. It is an interesting choice of figures, because in my perception a wizard and a lion are both strong, powerful and could be dangerous. On the other hand, I always imagined a dolphin and a butterfly to be beautiful, gentle and inspirational. They both have a sort of freedom of movement. As I am talking, I have just realized that the four characters represent the four elements: fire, air, earth and water. In that sense, it feels quite exciting to me, as if all bases are covered. I wonder if it has the same feeling for you?
>
> Please consider what we have all said, and work with any of the feedback that is useful for you. You don't have to accept everything we have suggested!

The aim of the feedback when doing creative supervision is to stimulate the supervisees to find their own answers. It is not to provide answers or to interpret in the manner of an expert. Even a clumsy, misdirected suggestion can help them clarify what is *not* happening, so long as it is offered as a possibility that they can discard, if they so wish. Returning to Heron's (1990) interventions, the feedback should be facilitative, using catalytic, cathartic or supportive interventions. It is not useful to use authoritative interventions such as prescriptive, informative or confrontative at this stage.

5. DISCUSSION AND ACTION PLAN

The feedback from the supervisor or other group members naturally evolves into dialogue and discussion. By now the supervisees have completely come out of their quiet, reflective or dreamy state, where they were accessing their intuitive knowledge. They become totally alert, and engage in critical thinking. In terms of the left- and right-brain model, they have moved from right to left.

The supervisees might want to discuss their process, but you should encourage them to focus on their learning rather than reiterating the original story. Sometimes creative supervision provides a sudden and cathartic understanding, but at other times further discussion is necessary. At this point you can use a wider range of Heron's (1990) interventions to help them.

In our experience it is often useful to conclude with an action plan. But this is not always necessary. Sometimes the understanding that has been gained is right-brained, intuitive and difficult to put into words. The supervisees might not be able to express themselves, but they say that something has changed inside. It might be that they are better at reflecting in action rather than on action, but it may also be because they have been through a non-verbal process. At these times it might be appropriate to do without an action plan, and wait and see if they cope differently with a similar situation in future. We would encourage them to note this in their journal and return to it again.

In some of the techniques we present in this book, the supervisee is encouraged at this point to go back into a second cycle of stages three to five. In other situations, the supervisor will be gently steering the supervisee towards making an action plan.

6. WRITING IN THE JOURNAL

You should encourage the supervisees to bring a reflective journal to every session, and create time for them to make notes or draw in it. Sometimes a camera or the camera function on a mobile phone is useful for photographing the work. A lot of the work done in creative supervision happens intuitively, in a slightly dreamlike state and does not use the conscious, thinking brain; it is therefore easy to forget. Because of this, we recommend that the supervisees make notes before they go home.

Although we are calling this the sixth stage, journal writing can occur at any point throughout the work (see Chapter 9).

7. ENSURING THAT SUPERVISEES COME OUT OF ROLE

Several of the methods and techniques described in this book involve role-play, or accessing the unconscious. In these circumstances, it is advisable to give the supervisee the space and time to come out of role and come back to the present. Of course, this will vary according to which technique you are using and how sensitive your supervisee is.

In some methods and techniques this is more necessary than in others. For example, meditation and visualization allows supervisees to access the unconscious or dreamlike state. They need to be told clearly, 'Allow yourself to gently come back to the present', or similar words. Frequently, they will be unable to continue with any discussion or critical thinking without de-roling first.

If they have been involved in role-play, often a change of chairs is enough to help them come out of role. Otherwise a clear statement of who they are in real life – for example, 'I am Tim!' – is a great way of coming back to the present. Another stronger statement would be 'I am not George, I am Tim!' Standing up for a moment also works. Another way is to do a quick brush down with the hands of the entire body, starting with the head and working down to the feet.

If the role-play has been through the use of toys or objects, ask the supervisee to break up the constellation. Remember the emotional investment that goes into these creations, and respect them. If you need to break up a constellation for someone else, then we suggest you ask permission first.

Using these seven stages of supervision creates a carefully boundaried and safe space in which the other person can work. These stages do not always need to be done in the same order. If you are working with a student or supervisee who is familiar with the process, some of the steps can be very brief.

Chapter 2

Becoming a Creative Supervisor

Creativity engages you in exploration. As a child you will have explored both through play and in learning. Perhaps you can recall your spontaneous and curious experimentation, some of which may have led to success while others may have ended disastrously. Were you a child who piled up inappropriately balanced books or bricks to stand on in order to reach a coveted treasure that was out of bounds? Perhaps you succeeded without anyone knowing. You may have been exploring how to make shapes in the sandpit or on the beach. Perhaps finding a milk bottle, you may have mixed sand with water and shaken the bottle hard until it broke and you were cut by the glass; receiving a reprimand. You might have been drawing a picture and wanted to share your excitement with a grown-up, but the person could not see, as you did, that this was an elephant. The inability of the grown-up to share your pleasure deflated your artistic enthusiasm.

Receiving negative responses to early creative exploration can leave its traces years after the event. Sadly this experience can be commonplace, stemming in the main from authority figures like parents or teachers.

These early experiences may make both the supervisor and supervisee feel reluctant to try creative methods of supervision. Engaging once again with the creative process may trigger childhood memories of struggling to be creative and being upset and/or embarrassed by negative feedback received for their efforts. When we refer to creative supervision, we are not talking about artistic talent but rather the ability to be spontaneous and to use imagination.

In this chapter, we explore how you can prepare yourself as a novice creative supervisor. We encourage you to do some self-supervision to free up any notions of not being good or creative enough. When you come to terms with your own creativity, you will be in a better position to encourage this in your supervisees. By mirroring your own ability to be creative as a supervisor, you are being congruent with the process that the supervisees will go through themselves.

Parallel process

We begin the chapter by demonstrating the importance of parallel process in our work. By parallel process we mean the mirroring process that happens when the dynamics, attitudes and characteristics of one interview become re-enacted in another one where the same material is being discussed. This mirroring can be usefully harnessed in supervision. If the supervisors perceive anything unusual in their interaction with a supervisee, they can use this to explore and cast light on the relationship that the supervisee previously had with the client. The supervisee unwittingly reproduces something of the original session. This can be portrayed by a gesture, an attitude or a feeling from the initial session that infiltrates the dynamic with the supervisor. Observing this phenomenon can deepen the understanding of the issue being brought by the supervisee.

Parallel process can also work in the other direction. The supervisor can model certain attitudes during supervision, which then become unconsciously repeated by the supervisees, when they meet again with their clients.

Hawkins and Shohet (1989), referring to parallel process, comment that:

> This function, which is rarely done consciously, serves two purposes for the supervisee. One is that it is a form of discharge – I will do to you what has been done to me and see how you like it; and the second that it is an attempt to solve the problem through re-enacting it within the here and now relationship. The job of the supervisor is to name the process and thereby making

it available to conscious exploration and learning, rather than to be submerged in the enactment of the process. (p.69)

CASE STUDY

Jane worked in an adult education institute for 18 years. When she began, she was the only person teaching her subject, and she could plan and write her own curriculum. Her teaching was observed once a year and, as long as the student feedback forms were satisfactory, she was more or less left to herself. Most of her students were interested in learning, and took part in the classes with enthusiasm. But once in a while there would be a student who was attention seeking, resistant or argumentative.

After about 12 years, her head of department recommended that all teachers should take part in the City and Guilds Teacher Training, which would be funded. Senior staff were to be the trainers. Jane joined the teacher training as a student, and was fascinated to observe that over the weeks discipline in the classroom disintegrated. All the students were mature students and experienced teachers, and should have known about good classroom behaviour. Maybe they had entered teacher training a little resentfully because of having to learn what they already knew, but in the first few lessons they were well behaved and respectful. After about three or four lessons, however, they started becoming cheeky, resistant or argumentative.

The teachers' in-training behaviour was paralleling that of their own students. It was their opportunity to act out some of the behaviour they had witnessed over many years, and find out how the senior staff would deal with it. It was as if they were aware that they did not need teacher training on the level of resources and techniques. But what they did need, and expressed unconsciously, was training in classroom management.

Parallel process reveals itself through behaviour, attitudes, body language, and the use of words and phraseology. In most supervision training, supervisors are encouraged to observe the supervisee, their own internal process, or the dynamic in the room, in order to check for parallel process.

In our experience, using the creative techniques to re-enact the client consultation is another form of parallel process. The advantage of using another medium is that supervisees can step back and become observers of their own creation. Using creative media allows them the opportunity to be external to it. For example, you might encourage supervisees to re-create a scenario from the consulting room or classroom using toys. The supervisees become engrossed in choosing toys that represent the characteristics of their clients or students. The choice of toys and placement of them reveals the dynamic of the relationship, and the atmosphere that was felt at the initial consultation. When the supervisees go into the discussion stage of the process, they can begin to decide how they would like to change that relationship.

If you are planning to include some creative supervision techniques, you should read through our recommended seven-stage process (see Chapter 1). If you feel confident and familiar with your own creativity, you can start right away. But if you feel some hesitation or reluctance to begin, we recommend that you explore your own creativity at home before you start. This will free you to act spontaneously in the moment, and help you to expand your abilities as a facilitator. Being a creative supervisor models expansive thinking to supervisees, and gives them permission and confidence to explore their issues in a creative way. It is another form of parallel process.

When you, the supervisor, go to your own supervisor, the parallel process will be re-created once again. It would be interesting to add to this experience by using the same creative techniques that you used with your supervisees (if your supervisor were interested in working in this way). We discuss these various techniques in later chapters.

Observe your own creativity

If you take time to observe yourself in your everyday activities, you may well find that you already have several activities or hobbies that include spontaneity or playfulness. Sometimes with these activities you can go into a calm, thoughtless space, where you just 'know' what to do. Examples of these could be walking your dog, digging the garden, playing with your children or grandchildren, cooking or experimenting with new recipes and ingredients, home decorating, sewing, knitting, DIY tasks, collecting sea shells, building sandcastles, skimming stones, flying a kite or editing your digital photos.

None of these activities in themselves is necessarily creative. It is the way that you engage with them that makes them so. For example, working in the garden can be done with care and consideration for the wildlife or for visual appeal. It can be a way of watching the seasons or preparing food for the table. Even though gardening tasks may be physically demanding, the gardener may feel stimulated by the work. The polar opposite would be the person who sees gardening as a series of chores to be done, such as cutting the lawn in the least possible time.

The person who just gets on with cutting the grass is task orientated and efficient. The one who puts their attention and affection into the garden becomes creative in their own right. We could say that the creative gardener is being expansive, in terms of body language and attitude. On the other side of the fence, the lawn cutter is being contractive, but may well express creativity elsewhere.

We suggest that you take some time to make a list of your everyday creative activities. You can write them into your notebook or reflective journal (see Chapter 9). Ask yourself the following questions:

- What do I enjoy doing that is intuitive, creative, spontaneous, stimulating or imaginative?

- What mood am I in while doing these things?

- How do I feel afterwards?

- How would I feel if there was no time for these activities?

Taking this one step further, we recommend that you do some experiential work with creative tasks to discover what you can learn from them.

The aim of these exercises is to reconnect you to the playfulness and spontaneity that you had as a child, and to show you how an act of creativity can lead to self-reflection. Experiencing this, rather than just reading about it, will increase your empathy and understanding as a supervisor. You will integrate both the intellectual and intuitive understanding of the process, and feel more confident as a facilitator of creative work.

EXPLORING YOUR OWN CREATIVITY

Choose any of the following exercises that appeal to you, and feel free to change them and develop them as you go along. There are no right or wrong ways of doing them. Just observe what happens to you and how you feel while you do them.

- *Make a doodle*: Get a large plain piece of paper (at least A4 or larger) and, using a soft pencil, scribble with large arm movements across the page.

  Sit back for a moment and then returning to the page see what images arise for you out of the doodles. Using felt-tipped pens or coloured pencils develop the picture. When you have come to a natural conclusion, review what you have drawn and see what it says about you.

- *Bubbles*: Collect up a large mixing bowl or washing-up bowl, some washing-up liquid, a straw, some watercolour paint or food colouring and several sheets of plain paper.

  Fill the bowl with water, and add the washing-up liquid and colouring. Blow through the straw to froth it up and create lots of bubbles. Place a sheet of paper on top of the bubbles and see what patterns it makes. Afterwards, reflect upon what it felt like to play with water and bubbles.

- *Pictures in the clouds*: Go for a walk and see what pictures you can see in the clouds or the trees. Let your imagination run free.

  On returning home, reflect on your moods and feelings at the time, and how you feel now.

- *Make a collage*: Collect up old newspapers, a blank sheet of A4 paper, scissors, pencils and glue. Cut out any pictures and headlines that appeal to you and put them together on the sheet of paper in any way that you wish. Glue them on.

  You will have made up a story board or vision board. What are you attracted to? What are you telling yourself?

- *Making faces*: Take several balloons and some felt-tipped pens. Experiment drawing a face on a fully blown-up balloon and one that has not been blown up; then blow it up. Enjoy the variety of faces that you create.

Notice the expressions that you gave the faces. What were your feelings while you worked? Consider what this means for you.

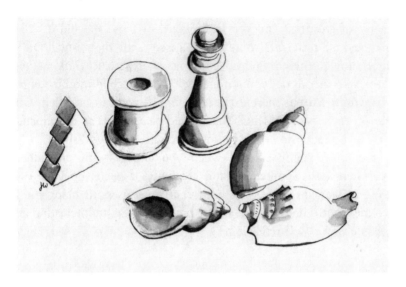

Figure 2.1 Shells and objets trouvés

- *Use household objects*: Collect a dozen or so small household objects – for example, bottle tops, corks, seashells, erasers, elastic bands, pen tops, dried beans, buttons or clothes pegs (see Figure 2.1).

  Now think of an incident that happened either last Christmas or on your summer holiday and represent it using your objets trouvés. Show the dynamic and interaction of what happened. Leave it for 30 minutes or more, and on returning to it observe it with fresh eyes. What can you learn from it?

- *A model house*: Go round your home collecting up materials that could be used for constructing a model house – for example, straws, paper, cardboard, boxes, matchboxes, toothpicks, glue, felt-tipped pens, scissors, paperclips, stapler.

  See what arises in you as you build your house.

USING YOUR REFLECTIVE JOURNAL

Notice your responses to doing these exercises. Afterwards it is worth spending a little time writing in your reflective journal about any thoughts or emotions that came up while you were doing them. Writing after playing helps you deepen your understanding of both the process and the results. What did you feel while you were in the process of creating? Did you feel relaxed or tense, excited or calm, energized or peaceful? Were you pleased with the result? Did it trigger any further thoughts, emotions or experiences? Sometimes these exercises can put you in touch with earlier childhood feelings.

Having tried out these exercises yourself, you can use them with your supervisees or students. They would be useful as an introduction to creative supervision or as warm-up exercises at a workshop.

It is our experience that when you engage with playfulness, experimentation, spontaneity and creativity, it opens up your own ability to work in more ways with your supervisees. It helps you to reconnect with the right side of the brain, and it is an interesting and dynamic way of self-reflecting.

Chapter 3

Opening up Unconscious Communication

Have you ever sat in a train looking around you? As you cast your eyes about, perhaps you feel a different sensation as you glance at one person in particular. It is a fleeting sensation, which is hard to verbalize, but a sense that this person resonates with you in a way that is different from the other people. If you were to analyze this further you might find that there is something particular to this person; it could be body build, a gesture, clothes or tone of voice that reminds you of someone you know. This will happen to all of us at some point even if we don't analyze what is happening. It is an unconscious process that occurs at different times in our lives. It is replicated in supervision and is what we explore in this chapter by looking at different sorts of unconscious interpersonal communication.

Unconscious communication takes place through body language, eye contact, facial expression, movements of the head, repeated gestures, tones of voice and autonomic responses. Mostly these are not consciously noticed by the other person but unconsciously they contribute to the type of relationship that is formed. In this chapter, we look at how you can become more observant of non-verbal communication, and harness its use in supervision. We look briefly at the unconscious processes including transference, counter-transference and the drama triangle. Finally, we look at some cases in which supervisors make only minimal interventions through responding to their own inner thoughts and feelings.

Listening on different levels

When teaching listening skills to novice practitioners, Jane asks them to consider non-verbal communication. They are encouraged to become aware of body language, eye contact, nods of the head, bodily noises, repeated gestures and the little 'hm-hm' noises that we make to express understanding without interrupting the other person's flow. Beyond this, Jane asks students to think about what else they do while listening. Most of us multi-task while listening, and maybe it is not humanly possible to listen while in a completely empty and receptive state.

Here are some examples of the other things that go on at the same time as listening:

- Making a clinical or intellectual assessment.

- Assessing according to previous ideas or prejudice.

- Making notes.

- Getting emotionally involved through pity or sympathy.

- Remembering a personal situation that parallels that of the speaker.

- Planning a response.

- Appearing to listen but too tired to concentrate.

- Appearing to listen, but focusing on going home, or the next meal.

If the aim of listening is to understand the other person better, then some of these other activities are going to be detrimental to that process. We can imagine a sort of sliding scale, with careful listening and focus on the speaker at one end of the scale while at the other end there is little or no focus on the speaker and the listener's thoughts are involved elsewhere.

However, we can take it a step further. The human brain is capable of complex tasks, and multi-tasking. If supervisors can be neutral observers of their own thought processes, if they can witness what is happening within their own brain and body, and notice at what level they are listening, then they have gained another supervision tool.

Hawkins and Shohet (1989) offer a process model of supervision. They identify six ways of analyzing what occurs in a psychotherapeutic supervision setting. These are: reflecting on the content of the therapy session; exploring the therapist's strategies and interventions; exploring the therapy process and relationship; focusing on the therapist's counter-transference; looking at the here and now process as a mirror of the there and then and, lastly, focusing on the supervisor's own counter transference. Here in the last of these Hawkins and Shohet suggest:

> The supervisor primarily pays attention to their own here-and-now experience in the supervision; what feelings, thoughts, and images the shared therapy materials stirs up in them. The supervisor uses these responses to provide reflective illumination for the therapist. The unconscious material of the therapy session which has been unheard at the conscious level by the therapist may emerge in thoughts, feelings, and images of the supervisor. (p.58)

The therapist or practitioner receives both conscious and unconscious information from the client. Conscious information can be verified with a voice recorder or typed notes. But unconscious knowledge – the things that they don't know that they know – can only be discovered through careful self-reflection or through the process of supervision.

When supervisors rather than supervisees observe their own inner processes during a session, this is a different way of unearthing the unconscious information. This is accepting that material can leapfrog from client to supervisor, while the supervisee is the unconscious carrier of this material. If you as supervisor can be a witness to your own inner processes, you can notice when you have responses that are unusual. If you find yourself with a thought, feeling or attitude that is stronger than normal, out of context, or unusual in any other way, it has probably arisen out of the supervisory material. This can be tentatively shared with the supervisee as a potentially useful piece of information.

PHYSICAL REACTIONS

Sometimes the story brought by a client, patient or supervisee creates a small but noticeable physical reaction in the therapist, practitioner or supervisor. For example, some of us might have experienced a slight prickling of the hairs on the back of the neck in response to hearing someone else's good news or success. Other responses might be a slight breathlessness or tightness in the chest, chilliness, restless feet or parallel pains to the client during the consultation. All these can happen face-to-face with a patient. They can equally happen at one remove, while the supervisee is talking about a patient or client.

These spontaneous physical reactions can be used as an effective supervision tool, if you notice them and feed them back to the supervisee. However, they need to be used quite tentatively. They are only useful if they resonate with the supervisees, enabling them to understand themselves or their client more completely. Sensitive and low-key offerings of the self are recommended – for example, 'I suddenly felt cold when you said that, and I wonder if that's relevant to the case' or 'Would it be useful to you to hear how I am feeling after hearing your story?'

EMOTIONAL REACTIONS

At other times, the reaction to the supervision material is emotional, and you need to do a quick reality check to decide whether it is one of your perennial buttons that has been pushed, creating a normal reaction for you; or whether this has come from the supervision material.

CASE STUDY

Jane was trying out a new supervisor, and negotiated to visit her once a month for three months. She brought a case of a man who had spoken freely and honestly in the consultation. He described himself as never relaxed, always having tunnel vision, wanting to work every hour, always on the phone growing his business. He said:

> I can't let them screw me. I have to be the one who comes out on top. I negotiated to buy a shop from a foreigner, and he was messing me about, so I went to the shop and kicked the door in and gave him a good hiding.

The case continued with graphic details of bullying and abuse.

The reason why Jane wanted to take this to supervision was that the man's delivery had been light-hearted, inviting collusion. Jane felt completely safe with him, and was unaware that she was possibly vulnerable to bullying from him herself. She enjoyed his story, as if it were a comedy thriller on TV, and encouraged him to talk. Afterwards she felt very disturbed, and wanted to examine her feelings in supervision.

The supervisor listened to the story and announced forcefully, 'I'm feeling really angry.' The indignation came out quite strongly, and she erroneously observed that this must be a parallel process to what Jane was feeling. She went on to make some prescriptive suggestions about how to terminate the working relationship with this man.

Reflecting on this later, Jane realized that her supervisor had provided the strong emotions that were lacking in the consulting room. It would have been more useful, however, if the supervisor could have recognized that the anger she felt was most likely coming from the man himself, at one remove. Despite his deceptively cheerful delivery, everything he described revealed a lot of anger. If the supervisor could have labelled this dissonance and offered it as a cool observation, rather than a heated and emotive reaction, it would have been useful for both of them to work through the complexity of the case, and decide on an action plan.

Wosket (1999), in her book *The Therapeutic Use of Self: Counselling Practice, Research and Supervision*, makes an interesting distinction between sympathy, empathy and compassion in relation to the use of self. She sees sympathy as a purely emotional reaction that is disempowering to the therapist or practitioner because it robs the person of the ability to think and act clearly. Empathy allows a bit more objectivity, so that the therapist can give helpful feedback in terms of providing a symbol or an 'as if' metaphor. This reflecting back in a slightly different form can help the client understand the issue. However, it can be a little bit cool, controlling and limited to the therapist's own experience.

Compassion on the other hand takes the therapist even further, having a 'quality of engagement and investment in the relationship' (Wosket 1999, p.213):

> In compassion the experiencing of emotion proceeds, but does not preclude, the ability to think and act as sympathy often does. When I experience compassion I am hit first by my feelings as a response to whatever is going on to the client, and may need to allow those to form more fully before I can make sense of them sufficiently to make a verbal response. I may experience a shudder, a lump in my throat, a lurch in my stomach, the sense of tears welling up, the sensation of coldness or hotness, the feeling of heaviness or of lightness, a sense of nausea or panic. Frequently there will be a feeling of being struck dumb in that instance as if the strength and impact of the feeling have momentarily robbed me of my ability to say anything meaningful. After that the thinking comes and may produce words that are clumsy and tentative as I struggle to give form to my feeling and offer it to my client. (p.213)

INCREASING YOUR AWARENESS OF NON-VERBAL COMMUNICATION

Here are three exercises that will help you increase your awareness of non-verbal communication.

- *Soap opera*: You can watch a soap opera with the sound turned off. Just watch the body language, gestures, facial expression and eye contact. It is easier to do this with a soap opera rather than a film, because the acting is exaggerated. See how much you can learn about the conversation or the plot before turning the sound back on.

- *Listening in*: If you are in a position to sit at the edge of a conversation, overhearing it but not expected to join in, you can practise observing on what level you are listening. For example, listening to children playing might be a useful exercise. Notice if you are totally focused or if your mind is drifting. Are you making an assessment or planning to answer back? Do you have an emotional or a physical reaction?

- *Observe a partner.* Sit or stand opposite someone who is prepared to work with you. Without talking, mirror or mimic each other for five minutes. You will need to observe each other carefully, and move when the other person does. You will notice that the longer this exercise goes on, the more you will become attuned to the minutest changes in your partner's breathing, movements and gestures. Your eye contact will be very steady, and you will also become acutely aware of each other's bodily noises.

Unconscious processes

An awareness of unconscious processes can enrich your understanding of case dynamics. Transference and counter-transference are unconscious processes that can occur in any therapeutic encounter. Transference happens when something in the current relationship unconsciously triggers a resonance for the supervisee or client with a past relationship. They then respond to the present situation in the way that they would have responded to the past one. This past relationship can be with anyone at all and need not have any connection to any therapeutic encounter. Often it is in relation to a perceived authority figure. Sometimes the transference can express itself as an over-warm and loving response to the supervisor or therapist, and at other times it may be expressed as feelings of anger, hostility or resentment.

Counter-transference is the name given to unconscious feelings felt by the therapist or practitioner towards the client or patient. If the practitioner starts to behave in a way that is different with this client, compared to the others, it might be as a result of counter-transference. Any strong feeling that seems out of keeping with the situation might be triggered by counter-transference and would benefit from being examined in supervision.

CASE STUDY

Caroline had a patient who repeatedly turned up late for her appointments. She would come in and say, 'I'm sorry I am late. You aren't angry with me, are you?' Caroline always replied, 'No, it is fine. I understand that it is hard for you to get here on time.' After a time, Caroline decided to examine this more deeply in order to understand what might be going on between her and the patient in this situation. The patient had a history in which she had found authority figures frightening. Caroline wondered whether unconsciously the patient was associating her with other frightening authority figures from the past who had told her off.

Had the relationship been a therapeutic one rather than a homeopathic one, the therapist would have worked with the transference, helping the client understand the nature of it. In this example, Caroline chose to respond in an unchallenging way, remaining unattached and neutral. She was aware of how important it was for the client that her response should not mimic that of the authority figures in the past because this would be detrimental to her relationship with the client.

Here is another example of how the unconscious process of transference can influence the practitioner-patient relationship.

CASE STUDY

A practitioner contracted to come to Jane for regular supervision. One session he brought a case that he wanted to discuss. The patient had a deep pathology and wasn't getting better as fast as either of them would have liked. The practitioner was thinking of asking the patient to stay on for another few months to see if a better prescription could be found. He wanted advice about how to support the patient, if she chose to stay.

Jane asked more about the case, and discovered that the patient was negative and complaining, with a strong sense of the unfairness of life. Her friends and the people at her work didn't treat her as well as she thought they should. In some respects, she was demanding and egotistical. Jane asked more about the relationship between the practitioner and the patient, and the practitioner said, 'I feel helpless. She says that the symptoms are so bad and she is so unlucky that she doesn't expect results.' They began to see that the patient had low expectations of the practitioner, transferring her attitudes and experiences from all previous therapeutic relationships onto this present relationship.

Identifying the unconscious processes made it easier for the practitioner to decide upon an action plan. It would not be appropriate to discuss the transference itself with the client, because this was not a psychotherapeutic relationship. But having insight into the dynamic enabled the supervisee to feel more empowered and less helpless. Together with Jane, he formulated an action plan in the event of the patient's returning.

The drama triangle

Another dynamic that is played out in supervision is that of the drama triangle. This configuration was first discussed by Karpman (1968) in his ground-breaking article 'Fairy tales and script drama analysis' (pp.39–43).

The three roles suggested by Karpman are victim, persecutor and rescuer. In brief, victims act out a role of helplessness, complaining and dependency. Their theme tune is 'it's not fair', but they are not good at taking advice, and might, in transactional analysis terms, play out the 'yes but' game. Persecutors are people who are angry and aggressive and enjoy conflict. They have fixed ideas about right and wrong, and are quite selfish. Rescuers are patient, understanding, responsible, placating and avoid conflict. They put others first, sometimes feeling taken for granted or guilty because of their unrealistic expectations. These are all polarized positions. In any interaction people will move between positions although most people have a preferential position (see Figure 3.1).

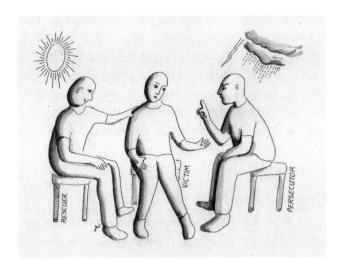

Figure 3.1 Three people as rescuer, victim and persecutor

We frequently see the drama triangle being played out in supervision groups. For example, a supervisee complains about a client, who appears to be pushing boundaries. The client does not come to appointments, or forgets to pay, or is unnecessarily aggressive, for example. In this scenario, the client is seen as a persecutor and the supervisee as the helpless victim. Then another group member steps in as rescuer, with a manner that is sympathetic and reassuring, completing the drama triangle. The rescuing intervention in a supervision group like this prevents the victim from learning from their experience. As facilitator, you have to be careful not to get drawn into a further re-enactment of the triangle. The supervisee might want to see you as another persecutor, or might try on the role of persecutor themselves to see what it feels like. It is useful to remain in the role of leveller.

Virginia Satir (1988) was a family therapist who developed the position of the leveller. She wrote about different modes of behaviour that she termed placator, blamer, computer, distractor and leveller. Of the leveller, she says in her book *The New Peoplemaking*:

> People who are levelling show an integration, a flowing, an aliveness, an openness and what I call a juiciness. Levelling makes it possible to live in a vibrant way, rather than a dead way. You trust these people and you know where you stand with them and you feel good in their presence. Their position is one of wholeness and free movement. (p.94)

In the role of leveller, you can be centred, honest and authentic, without assumptions or projections. You can be quietly assertive, without being aggressive, and you can be flexible. This is perhaps easier to do if you are the facilitator of a group, observing three other people playing out the drama triangle. If you are caught up in the dynamics of the triangle, your inner witness needs to be present, to notice what is happening. Then you can move over to become the leveller.

Creating a sacred space

One advantage of understanding non-verbal communication is that it can be used deliberately to create a good working environment for a consultation, supervision session or tutorial. By working environment, we mean the dynamic of the relationship or interpersonal process, and we suggest that it extends beyond the relationship of the people working together, forming a protective bubble around them. This can be seen in a workshop environment where students are asked to work in small groups. Some groups are self-conscious, glancing around the room or giggling. Other groups create an internalized focus that enables them to do deep and effective work without noticing the hum of other people in the room. They manage to re-create the 'sacred space' of the consulting room, where the client can feel truly heard.

A good working environment is created in several different ways. We always recommend that you start with a clear contract and have appropriate boundaries. The room in which you meet should be comfortable and suitable for confidentiality. You should be mentally and emotionally open and present.

Body language can be studied and used as a tool to enhance the working relationship. Your conscious use of gentle, non-aggressive body language, with appropriate eye contact, will build up trust and confidence in your supervisee, student or client. Your ability to read their non-verbal signals will enable you to make decisions about how best to communicate with them.

You should aim for a state of balance between genuine interest in the person in front of you, and awareness of your own inner state. The other person should feel supported, appreciated, respected and listened to, which in turn enables them to open up.

The minimum intervention

We have suggested that you should aim to be totally present and alert, listening to and observing the other person, aware of non-verbal communication and your own inner processes. But you don't always need to do much; and sometimes the minimum intervention is more potent than a long discussion. This is not the same as being passive, or absent-minded. It is not an aggressive silence either, challenging the supervisee to speak. It is a state of calm and gentle regard with a clear awareness of boundaries.

Using minimal intervention can take courage, because for many supervisors the natural impulse may be to respond in an active way – for example, to be prescriptive or informative. Sometimes supervisors have agendas of their own and will want to 'solve' the problem following their own hypothesis. This will be frustrating for the supervisee and will not lead them to find their own insights. To create the space for the supervisee or group to learn, without controlling them through words, means doing less and trusting in outcomes. Sometimes non-verbal supervision arises spontaneously, as in the following case example.

CASE STUDY

Jane was privileged to observe a neat piece of non-verbal supervision while studying in a supervision workshop. She was working in a triad, and she had the role of observer. The storyteller was becoming quite long-winded about her client. Jane felt restless and wished the storyteller would get to the point. She began to feel critical of the supervisor in the triad, who appeared to be not managing the session very well. She turned her attention to him and began to observe him more closely. He had begun the session with his head on his hand in a listening pose, three fingers curled on the cheek, with the index finger open. Gradually he began to use the whole hand to support his head, and his head began to droop. Then his arm suddenly fell off the armrest of the chair, and his head collapsed completely.

The storyteller had been unobservant of her supervisor, because she was involved in her story. But the abruptness of his arm falling off the armrest, mimicking someone falling asleep, brought her to a halt. 'Oh,' she said, 'I'm going on too long aren't I? That is exactly what my patient was doing. I felt exhausted when I was working with her.'

As the three of them debriefed on what had happened, the supervisor apologized for being rude, but said he felt he wanted to follow his own intuition and react physically rather than use verbal interventions.

If you are running a group, your role as facilitator is to maintain boundaries of time, communication and relationship. If the group has been meeting regularly for some time, and everyone is familiar with the group contract and house rules, then you can be less active. Your interventions can become minimal, and even reduced to non-verbal signals to the group at times. Smiling, nodding and leaning forward can be enough to show the group that they are on track.

CASE STUDY
Caroline writes:

> My group met in the beginning of January. They started with expressing their frustrations and anxieties around home life, work, and particularly the recent redundancies and redeployments in the department. Normally appreciations are shared. One group member shared his appreciation of the snow and the fact that the email had been down for a month. The group talked about the peace and quiet of the snow; and the family time over Christmas with food and cooking.
>
> The group wanted to chat, and were not interested in the usual tasks of supervision. They wanted to digress and talk about gardens. From time to time I checked in to see if everyone was okay with this because one of the members of the group had said that she had an issue that she wanted to explore. But they all decided that they wanted to carry on. I let them.
>
> I noticed how hard that was for me. I was torn between thinking this is not my task as facilitator, and being totally intrigued by what was emerging. Now they were talking about allotments and this led to dreams of what they could grow there. The talking was organic and the ideas evolved. Someone mentioned how during the snowy period she had shopped for her elderly neighbours. She was shocked that this had not happened for her own elderly parents who had been snowed in for days. There was talk of street parties and the idea of reconnecting with our environment. The theme of quality of life was emerging and the need for nourishment. The amalgamation of two departments and with it a number of redundancies and redeployments had left most people feeling vulnerable and fragmented. Nourishment seemed to be a good place to start.
>
> The idea was suddenly born of inviting everyone in the newly formed department to a pot-luck lunch with home-grown

or home-cooked produce. Someone volunteered to design the invitations. There was a sigh of relief as if tension had dropped away.

This session had a different feel to it from sessions where everyone was trying to solve the problems inherent in the amalgamation of two disparate departments. Here, through conversation, laughter and dreaming, the idea of community was emerging. Without any prompting, the group had gone from a complaint about the department to an organic brainstorming, through to an action plan. I hardly did any active supervision. I just joined in the talk about allotments.

In this case example, Caroline held the space for the group, checking in with them before allowing them to go off task; and she checked in with her own inner process as well. She created an atmosphere that enabled 'conversation, laughter and dreaming', and finally an action plan.

Increasing your awareness of non-verbal communication

Unconscious interpersonal communication takes place within many different sorts of relationships. It occurs through body language, eye contact, facial expression, nods or shakes of the head, repeated gestures, tone of voice and the choice of words used. If you can increase your awareness of these, you can start to use them within supervision, as well as in other relationships. We suggest that there will always be some part of non-verbal communication that remains unconscious. But you can train yourself to become alert to some of the messages that have been sent unconsciously to you, and choose whether and how you want to use them. Conversely, you can control some of the non-verbal messages that you are sending out to a client or supervisee, and consciously create the best possible environment for them.

Chapter Four

Using Toys and Bricks

We are surrounded in our everyday world with representational symbols. Take, for example, exclamation marks. As a road sign this signals danger to us, while in another context it would read as a part of speech. An apple might have the connotation of the computer company or the Big Apple of New York. Objects, icons and logos come to have multi-meanings that enrich our understanding of life around us. Some of the meanings are conscious and others unconscious. The advertising industry is masterly in the way in which it extends into the unconscious resonances when it chooses an image for its maximum impact. Just as symbolism is used in our environment, it can be used in supervision as a powerful tool to access unconscious meanings in our work.

In this chapter, we discuss the use of toy animals, figurines and bricks to help open up the unconscious understanding of supervisees and enable them to reflect further. It is a method of supervision that uses symbolic objects to represent people, their emotions and interactions. They are placed in a configuration, and re-assessed to find out what is being unconsciously expressed.

A more conventional mode of supervision might involve the verbal presentation of an issue followed by a discussion. Sometimes talking through the story with a supervisor is enough to find a deeper understanding. At other times, repeating the story can act as a smokescreen, preventing the supervisee from discovering anything further about the situation. It is in the nature of stories that they change with the retelling. Using symbolic personae to represent the protagonists in a story allows the supervisees to re-view the situation, seeing it again with fresh eyes. This physical and visual externalization of what happened is what allows them to deepen their understanding of the original situation.

Another advantage of using toys and animals is that the process can be much quicker than talking through all the details of the issue or critical incident. It can also work beautifully when used as a re-supervision, when the first exploration of the issue did not produce enough insights. The first exploration of the issue might have been in the reflective journal or with a colleague, and this has value in itself. The second exploration, if it uses creative supervision, can add to the depth of understanding. This technique can be used both in one-to-one supervision and in group work.

The symbolic value of animals and figurines

Animals can be used to personify different aspects of human nature. These symbolic images come up again and again in literature, fairy stories and mythology – for example, in Aesop's fable, *The Fox and the Crow*, the crow is represented as naïve and the fox as cunning, sly and devious:

> A Fox once saw a Crow fly off with a piece of cheese in its beak and settle on a branch of a tree. 'That's for me, as I am a Fox,' said Master Reynard, and he walked up to the foot of the tree. 'Good-day, Mistress Crow,' he cried. 'How well you are looking today: how glossy your feathers; how bright your eye. I feel sure your voice must surpass that of other birds, just as your figure does; let me hear but one song from you that I may greet you as the Queen of Birds.' The Crow lifted up her head and began to caw her best, but the moment she opened her mouth the piece of cheese fell to the ground, only to be snapped up by Master Fox. 'That will do,' said he. 'That was all I wanted. In exchange for your cheese I will give you a piece of advice for the future. "Do not trust flatterers."'

Potter (1908), in *The Tale of Jemima Puddleduck*, depicts the fox in the same way.

Some of the symbolic meanings and values attached to animals are universal archetypes. The same imagery can be seen around the world.

For example, young animals can symbolize innocence, sweetness or cuddliness; dinosaurs can represent power, strength or the magical abilities of a dragon. But other symbolic interpretations seem to vary from culture to culture, so we recommend that you always check with supervisees what imagery or symbolism each animal or figurine has for them.

In Britain, animal imagery has entered everyday language and adds richness to its meaning. We might refer to a person as a wet fish, a tiger or a pussy cat, a bitch or a fat cow, a fat cat or the pejorative fat toad. We might talk about a venomous tongue, a memory like an elephant, or weaving webs like a spider. We speak about being treated like a dog, or looking hangdog. We accredit the dolphin with intelligence and the bull with anger. People may be referred to as parroting or rabbiting on, being as quiet as a mouse, scared as a cat, going at a snail's pace, or being as busy as a bee. We refer to the wise owl, the cheeky monkey, the cuddly bear or a sheep in wolf's clothing.

When we use plastic toy people in supervision, we are tapping into different aspects of human nature that are represented either in a life-like or a caricatured way. For example, the witch figure is an ugly, crooked caricature of an elderly woman wearing black and symbolizing evil and malicious power. A younger woman, in a white dress with yellow hair, carrying a wand, is ambiguous, halfway between the white witch and the princess. The queen is stately and beautiful, representing power, control or feminine strength. The wizard, with his strong upright stature and flowing beard, has qualities of power or the misuse of power as well as wisdom and knowledge. Folk dolls with plaits and aprons are sometimes seen as figures of innocence, honesty and naïveté. The soldier, depending on his stance and armaments, represents aggression or protection. The fire-fighter shows energy and quick thinking with heroic qualities ready to rescue and save the day. The robot can be a figure of fun, or represent a mindless automaton.

VARIETY AND DEPTH IN SYMBOLISM

We can take this further by looking at dogs as an example to show the variety and depth of the symbolic content. Dogs are used as guide dogs, police dogs, sheep dogs, guard dogs, hunting dogs and in some cultures may be seen as man's faithful friend. Traditional stories and urban myths abound with stories about faithful dogs. One story of a dog who was faithful to his master beyond the grave is that of Greyfriar's Bobby. This Skye terrier was so devoted to his master John Gray, even in death, that for 14 years he lay on John Gray's grave, only leaving for food.

In myth, religion and fairy stories, dogs can be considered good. Cooper (1978), in his book *An Illustrated Encyclopaedia of Traditional Symbols*, suggests that 'The dog sometimes accompanies the Good Shepherd and he is usually a companion of healers such as Aesculapius, and all hunters and mother goddesses, the mother goddess often being called "the bitch" and portrayed as the whelping bitch' (p.52).

In real life, dogs have been trained to be helpful towards man. Yet in language we can often use the metaphor of a dog in a very negative way, implying second-class citizenship, or worse. Dog-inspired language includes calling someone a bitch, cur, hangdog, or having a tail between their legs.

In mythology, dogs play a key role, and the black dog can represent sorcery and diabolical powers. Caspari and Robbins (2003), in *Animal Life in Nature, Myth and Dreams*, suggest that:

> Given their instinct to guard, dogs have been long associated with guarding real thresholds. So, it seems symbolically apt that one be placed at the boundary between the world of the living and that of the dead. A Greek goddess, Hecate, who had power over heaven, earth and sea and presided over magic and spells, is associated with dogs; she is identified with the original hell-hound, Cerberus, the three headed dog that guards the gates of Hades. (p.82)

Using bricks with the figurines

We recommend including bricks when working with animals and figurines because they help create the platform or stage for the figures. We find it useful to work with small bricks of irregular size and painted in different colours. Symbolically, bricks are to do with structure and the potential for building. When a few bricks are put together, they create a wall, a house or a plinth. Bricks can be used to symbolize a boundary or fence, or to separate or interconnect different areas.

The placing of the bricks is an important part of the work. Their height in relation to each other and in relation to the animals and figurines can create and show different dynamics of a situation. Sometimes supervisees will choose to work only with animals and figurines, even though bricks have also been offered. This can be significant in their story. The absence of bricks may mean an absence of boundaries, or an absence of a sense of place or space.

Figure 4.1 Owl, fox, sheep and dog

CASE STUDY

Animals and bricks were used when a practitioner came to us wanting to discuss a confrontation that happened with her line manager at work. We asked the practitioner to make a representational scene. This is loosely represented in the drawing (see Figure 4.1):

> *The practitioner chose a large fox for the line manager and a small owl for herself. Then she put in a sheep, a bear and several dogs behind the manager/fox, and built a brick wall behind herself/owl. When the practitioner was satisfied with the constellation, the supervisor described what she saw: 'The owl appears to have its back to the wall, while the fox has a supportive and strong team behind it. It seems to me the owl is in a difficult position.' These observations allowed the practitioner*

to reflect further on the dynamics shown there. The supervisor then asked the practitioner if there was anything she would like to change in the constellation. After some deliberation she put the owl on the top of the wall overlooking the manager/fox and its team. The supervisor asked what that felt like, and she said 'Much better. I feel lighter, a sense of relief.' We then discussed the symbolism of her choice of animals. She made a connection between her choice of the fox and the devious nature of her line manager. (Schuck and Wood 2007, p.25)

The practitioner was able to go back to her work and make some subtle shifts that enabled her to feel better in relation to her line manager. She no longer felt hemmed in by the manager and could take a wider bird's eye view of the situation. We could have discussed an action plan, and made suggestions about how she dealt with the manager in future. In this instance we did not (see Chapter 1). Increasingly we have found that if change has been made on the unconscious level, it does not always need to be vocalized or written. The unconscious change will automatically manifest new behaviour the next time supervisees find themselves in the same situation.

The beauty of using such a direct and visual description of a dynamic means that the new perception enacted out in the constellation then frequently becomes paralleled in real life. We suggest that working this way can change the attitude of supervisees that underpins all their thoughts, emotions and actions. Changing their attitude means that they will approach the people they work with in a different way in future, without having to plan the details of what they will say to them.

FACILITATING A SESSION USING TOYS AND BRICKS

Generally, supervisees come into supervision prepared with something they wish to work with. They might bring a critical incident with a patient, client, team leader or colleague; or they may bring aspects of their work such as their professional development that they want to explore further.

We suggest that you encourage your supervisees to begin by summarizing their topic in a sentence or two in the manner of a headline, rather than starting the topic immediately. Once you have established what the content will be, you can negotiate with them about what sort of method they wish to use. If they are interested in using toys, it is an exciting way of expanding their understanding of any particular issue. Even if they are resistant, our suggestion is that all supervisees should experiment using animals and bricks at least once. Explain to them that it does not take much time, it can be fun and there are no right or wrong answers. However, it is best to negotiate with them over this; creative supervision does not work if it is imposed.

Start the process by giving them clear instructions to choose animals, figurines and bricks to represent all aspects of their issue, and to place them carefully into a configuration that represents the whole picture. Usually the toys are used to re-enact scenes that have happened, in order to encourage self-reflection. At other times the toys create scenes that the supervisee would like to happen, as a positive visualization. We refer to this configuration as a constellation.

You should discourage supervisees from talking in detail about their issue. They can briefly introduce it, or just begin the work without an introduction. Talking can be a useful and reflective way of working but it can keep the supervisees in their story, describing what happened, rather than exploring deeper issues. When they enter into this process of re-enactment through the symbolic animals, they are retelling the story by unconsciously projecting their feelings about the situation. It is best if they are left to do this in silence.

The issue can be anything at all. When we first started working this way, we used the animals and figurines to represent people, such as patients, clients, colleagues, managers or other professionals. But we soon realized this could be expanded so that animals and figurines can also represent emotions, aspects of a character, or objects such as a book, money or anything else that comes into the story. Objects should not be represented literally, with the toy as the image of reality; instead they should be represented symbolically, revealing their emotional value for the supervisee. For example, a book could be represented by a wise owl, an evil wizard or a smiling friend.

CREATING THE CONSTELLATION

At times, we have observed that supervisees enter an internalized state while choosing the elements of the constellation. You need to respect this and observe it in silence. When they are engaged in playing with the toys, quietly and with no interruptions, they tap into their unconscious processes. Sometimes you will notice that they make a quick choice, but at other times their hand will hover over many animals; occasionally a first choice is rejected, and a new participant chosen. Equal care is taken in placing the participants. Some supervisees verbalize their process and some remain in silence. Supervisees are very clear about what feels right, as if following some instinct that cannot be over-ridden. It is important that you as facilitator, or any other observers, remain completely silent during this process.

Once all the figures are chosen and placed in a constellation and the supervisee is satisfied with the result, you can initiate the next step, which is giving feedback. We recommend that you simply describe what you observe from your own perspective. For example, 'I notice there are very large animals on one side of the fence and very small animals on the other side of the fence', or 'I notice all the animals you have chosen are wild animals rather than tame animals'. You can also give very gentle and totally owned interpretation – for example, 'From where I am sitting it looks like the fox is going to eat the chicken', 'In my personal mythology a fox is quite sly, I wonder whether this applies to your fox', or 'I was interested to note that the polar bear got exchanged for a teddy bear while you were working'.

CASE STUDY

A teacher wanted to explore her teaching in different groups and settings. She taught in three establishments and felt that she worked in a different way in each of them. The supervisor encouraged her to choose an animal to represent her in each of her teaching situations. She chose a tiger cub, a turquoise parrot and a sheep dog. She talked as she was placing these animals, saying, 'With this first group I am a tiger with teeth and claws but I am also quite playful as well. In the second group, I am a brightly dressed theatrical parrot who has a lot to say. In the third group, I am a sheep dog that organizes them.' In the background she put a robot, which she said was her 'worst nightmare'.

The supervisor gave feedback on this constellation.

> *All three aspects of your teaching that you have represented here seem to me to have a lot of energy. In my view, I would say that two of them, the dog and the parrot, are good communicators. The parrot and the tiger are very colourful, so I wonder if you put on a show when you are teaching. All three of them have sharp claws, strong teeth or a beak so I can imagine they would all be good with boundaries. They are completely different to the stiff and rigid robot, which puzzles me.*

The teacher explained that she despised teachers who gave lectures without thinking or interacting with the students. She suspected there was a lot of this sort of teaching in the establishments where she taught. She felt it was in the background, so this is where she put the robot. At the same time she admitted it might just be her prejudice. The supervisor suggested that she replaced the robot with something else, but instead the teacher chose a knight to stand in front of the robot and protect her from him.

The teacher was satisfied with the feedback, and felt more secure in her different teaching styles having reflected on them in this way. The supervisor encouraged her to make some notes in her journal on what she had discovered.

Lahad (2000) in *Creative Supervision,* says:

> The use of interpretation will be almost nil, unless requested by the supervisee. Most of the time, introspection and lateral reflection are encouraged as a way to jointly investigate the 'product'. At times we also use the gestalt approach of exploration and listening, such as personifying an object and letting it explore itself, its surroundings, etc. This is how we usually start our journey into creative explorations. (p.23)

While respecting what Mooli Lahad says, we have found that the use of gentle interpretation can be very useful, so long as it is totally owned by the supervisor and not imposed. As a supervisor, your personal understanding of mythology or symbolism could be completely different from that of your supervisees, because there are no universal truths. You should be authentic, restrained and respectful in your feedback. Your views, even if they do not resonate with the supervisees, will encourage their exploration, enabling them to understand the constellation for themselves. There are no right or wrong answers either for the supervisor or the supervisee, because the constellation is purely being used as a tool to enable reflection.

The supervisees enter a state in which they are almost unaware of the constellation they have created. They have been working instinctively, while you are observing from a more logical and thinking part of yourself. Your observations may refer to the choice and placing of animals and figurines – for example, 'I notice that the wizard and the cow are not looking at each other.' You might also make observations about the gestures and body language incorporated in the plastic figurines. When bricks are used as well, this adds another dimension, and you can give feedback on the positioning, colour and height of the bricks. For example, 'I notice there is a very high and precarious wall around that figure' or 'I notice you did not use any bricks, and to me this suggests that there might be an issue about boundaries.'

Following your observations, supervisees can become more dispassionate observers of the constellation they have just made and they can add their own observations. A dialogue ensues that helps to clarify the situation further. Deeper meanings are revealed, as both of you notice more and more about the position, eye contact, body language, domesticity, wildness, age or size of the animals and figurines. Nothing is held to be simply coincidence.

The final step of the process is to enable the supervisees to make changes to the choice of toys and bricks or the positioning of them. Sometimes this happens spontaneously and sometimes you need to ask them if they would like to make any changes. We have noticed that some supervisees can be quite resistant to developing or changing the constellation. They have represented the situation as it is and cannot conceive of anything different. This is a stuck position. However, modifying the constellation can cause a shift in the unconscious processes, and thereby transform the attitude, which in turn has an impact on the real-life situation. Reframing the constellation can be strong enough to clarify an action plan, or it can be gentle enough to create possibilities. Changes can be made consciously but even then they also bear the mark of the unconscious. Further discussion might ensue.

If supervisees refuse to make any changes, you can leave the constellation as it is. The act of creating it and looking at it has probably enabled some self-reflection. You can gently challenge the supervisees to find out why they are so attached to the current situation. This bears some exploration and the reasons will be personal. The supervisees may need to reflect further alone or they may have a fear of change.

Another tactic you might use for supervisees who are resisting changing the constellation would be to question them about the emotional factors behind the current choice. Then you can ask them to choose the opposite quality and find an animal or figurine that represents this. For example, weakness can become strength or power. The opposite quality figure needs to be placed within the constellation so that the supervisees feel the full impact. Alternatively you might offer to choose a new animal or figurine for them, just so that they can experience what it would feel like. These last two are directive interventions and are best done only when you have established a trusting, working relationship with a supervisee.

For some supervisees it is a relief to be able to consciously change the constellation. The first constellation with its feedback can bring enormous insights that leave supervisees impatient for change. Alternatively the process might leave them feeling vulnerable, exposed or out of control. Changing the constellation can give them an opportunity to feel in control again.

CASE STUDY

Jane wanted to explore an incident that happened to her outside her normal work hours. She writes:

> An artist had reluctantly agreed to visit a client who had had a stillborn baby the previous day, to take some photographs. When she arrived at the house, she was startled to find the client was cuddling the stillborn baby, something she had not expected. The following week, the artist began to tell me about it, clearly in need of debriefing and supervisory help. But the setting was informal and the artist was not one of my supervisees. The place

and the timing were inappropriate, so I backed off from helping her. Afterwards I regretted this, feeling uncomfortable and guilty.

When working with my supervisor, I chose to work with animals and bricks. I created a brick boundary fence in a loose figure of eight shape. Within one circle, the mother and baby were represented by a horse with its head looking down towards a small figurine, lying on its back with the feet in the air. Within the other circle, I placed myself, as a soldier bearing a standard, feet firmly planted, and covered in armour. For me, the standard represented my own high standards of supervisory practice, including clear contracting. Between these two circles, in the centre of the figure of eight, I placed the artist, represented as a small bear still looking towards the mother and baby. It was as if she could not stop looking towards them (see Figure 4.2).

Figure 4.2 Soldier, small bear, figurine and horse

I felt satisfied that this constellation represented the scene. I indicated to my supervisor that I would like to receive some feedback. My supervisor noted that the expression on the bear's face was almost of incredulity. I had not noticed this expression when I chose and placed the animal, but this paralleled the artist's shock. The supervisor also noticed that the Jane/soldier looked as though he was protecting the bear. The supervisor commented that he looked severe. These were interesting insights for me.

My supervisor noted the parallel process of the artist's reluctance to see the mother and my reluctance to do supervision with the artist. This was shown visually with the two different boundary fences that mirrored each other.

I decided I would like to make some changes to the constellation, because it felt uncomfortable to me. I opened up my boundaries by opening the figure of eight to create a sort of corridor through which the artist/bear could come towards me should it choose. I changed the bear into a calf. It was still a young animal, but this time it was larger and more in proportion to the other figures. It had more strength. I decided I did not want to change my own figure as a soldier bearing a standard. I still had my standards of contracting and boundaries. But I moved the soldier to one side of the boundary fence, allowing the artist/calf more space to come towards me.

My learning from this supervision was that I had not behaved badly towards the artist, which had been my fantasy. Representing her as a young bear, or a calf, made me see how she had lacked strength, both with her client and in asking me for help. I had responded with sympathy on a human level, but I had not chosen to give her more than this. Representing myself as a standard-bearer in every sense of the word reminded me that supervision only works well with clear contracting and clear boundaries. From this, I could work out a strategy, should something like this happen again in the future. I would contract for them to come to me for a proper supervision session.

The benefits of using animals and bricks

Working creatively when you are the supervisor or facilitator means you have to stand back, and trust the process. You will find that there is great potency for the supervisees in hearing your observations, and your gentle, owned interpretations. Even though you may not have had the satisfaction of hearing the story, they will get their needs met. In our experience, playing and fantasy can open a deeper understanding and influence changes in real-life situations.

According to supervisees' own learning styles, some will gravitate automatically towards creative supervision, while others, perhaps more logical and linear thinkers, will reject it. We recommend that you encourage all supervisees to try using animals, figurines and bricks at least once in order to get an experiential feel for how it works. This would enable them to be in a better position to decide what technique to use on a particular issue in the future.

Linear thinkers may find it harder to relate to this way of working. Caroline led a group of students through this exercise once and found there was one articulate and linear thinker who could readily create the constellation, but was unable to access the symbolic resonances of the figurines. Having chosen a wizard and a plastic figure in a hard hat to represent himself, he could see nothing but the objects themselves and, when Caroline offered her observations of the constellation, including a reference to the hard hat, the supervisee could not take this thought any further. This is a rare occurrence but it is possible that non-visual and non-spatial learners may not resonate with this particular creative exercise.

If you are uncertain about the value of working with toys and animals yourself, you could try this experiment. Choose an issue that you have already reflected on and discussed in supervision. Working with your supervisor or a colleague, follow the steps that we recommend and set up the same issue with an animal and bricks constellation. See what new insights you discover.

This method of supervision gives quick and often unexpected results because it uses symbolic objects to represent people, their emotions and their interactions. It is a quick way to get at unconscious processes. Often, once supervisees have tried this method, even reluctant supervisees, they opt for it time and time again. It cuts across the conscious processes and allows something new to emerge. There is an excitement and a playfulness attached to it that makes it feel less like work and more like fun, encouraging supervisees to return for more insightful sessions.

Chapter 5

Discovering Visualization, Metaphor and Drawing

If you have ever listened to children playing, you will know that they readily create their own realities through their imaginations. One child may organize dolls or soft animals in rows and act out the role of a teacher, another one may run around being a racing driver, yet another may crawl along the floor declaring themselves a snake. This ability to imagine and visualize starts early in life and then can lie dormant. In this chapter, we are going to show how the ability to visualize, use metaphor and drawings can be reawakened and harnessed to gain insights in supervision.

With many of the creative tools that we recommend in this book, supervisees are encouraged to temporarily let go of their thinking, logical and conscious brain and access their intuitive, imaginative and non-verbal intelligence. Visualization is probably the least logical and most intuitive of all the methods we write about.

There are two types of visualization that we would like to discuss. One is exploratory visualization. The aim of this is to understand the hidden influences on supervisees' actions and to open up some of their blind spots. The technique uses imaginative stories and pictures to access unconscious patterns. This can be done either through choosing a metaphor or through a full visualization. The other type of visualization is creative visualization, where the power of the imagination is used to create a new and positive outcome.

Exploratory visualization

Luft (1984) in his model, 'The Johari window', which he writes about in *Group Processes: An Introduction to Group Dynamics* (p.60), suggests that there are four different arenas of awareness, two of these relating to conscious knowledge and two to the unconscious. The open area is visible both to yourself and to others. It contains the habits, mannerisms, thoughts and emotions that everyone can observe. The hidden area contains information that you are aware of, but you choose to hide from other people. The other two arenas are unknown to you. The blind area can be seen by others and the unknown area is buried so that no one can see it. The process of supervision, which encourages supervisees to reflect on their hidden motivations and attitudes will enable them to open up some of their blind spots and also a proportion of their hidden area (see Figure 5.1).

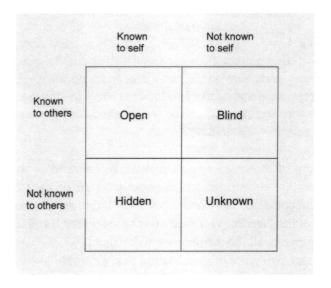

Figure 5.1 The Johari window

Exploratory visualization is a quick and effective way of reviewing what is already known, as well as accessing hidden information. For example, a verbal or written review is often just a list of what is already consciously known. The list contains familiar information and the oral or written form of presentation is equally well known and comfortable for supervisees. When a completely different model or method is used to look at the same information, the new viewpoint can open up interesting insights. Things that supervisees were avoiding, or hesitating to look at directly, reveal themselves through indirect methods.

USING METAPHOR AS EXPLORATORY VISUALIZATION

We will start with the use of metaphor, which is a simplified version of exploratory visualization. It can be quick and effective, and involves supervisees in using their imagination. It is useful as a way of initiating dialogue, or working with the reflective journal. Supervisees are asked to choose a metaphor to represent their work, their client or anything else that they might wish to work on. The metaphors themselves need to feel right to the supervisees, though it usually takes some questioning, discussion or challenge to reveal the full story. However strange a metaphor may appear, it is important that you respect it and help the supervisee understand it more deeply.

CASE STUDY

Jane was setting up a new supervision group with four independent and experienced practitioners. They were interested in group work, but had not worked with each other before. Jane spent some time with them, contracting generally and negotiating ground rules for the group. They agreed to treat each other with respect, listen carefully, and give fair and balanced feedback. Everything was in place for a good beginning, but Jane decided she wanted to start them off with a group exercise that would build up trust. She asked them if they would do a short group exercise. She invited them to sit quietly, think about the private practice that each of them was involved in and choose the metaphor that best described it. 'For example you could say, my practice is like a runaway train, a sleeping cat, or a circus juggler.'

After everyone had chosen their metaphor, Jane suggested that they present it to the person sitting on their right, who would challenge them to think further. This would continue around the circle. One practitioner said, 'I feel I'm on the edge, perhaps the edge of a cliff, and I cannot decide which way to go.' Her colleague thanked her warmly for an interesting metaphor, and asked her to say more about 'which way to go'. The practitioner now described her practice as being a half-open door, and she was hesitating to go through it. Her colleague challenged, 'What is on the other side of the door?' She thought quietly for a while, and then began to talk about a fear of too much commitment and responsibility. Jane stopped her there because of time limitations, and suggested that she continued to work on this in the next meetings of the group.

In a situation like this, Jane could have asked everyone to introduce themselves, telling a bit about their personal history. The results would probably have been factual and numerical. (The year they graduated, the hours they worked or the numbers of patients on their books.) It would have been safe, and interesting, but it would not have revealed much about their practices or about themselves to each other.

Jane chose to work with metaphor as a way of building up trust and initiating group work. She gave clear examples of what she meant by a metaphor. The group understood what was wanted and, although they might have felt amused, stimulated or slightly resistant, nobody was completely out of their depth. Being given the opportunity to challenge each other around the circle provided equality. Having Jane there as facilitator created a safety net.

Each metaphor provided a springboard to the group's understanding, both in terms of the practitioners' understanding of themselves and the group members getting to know each other. Jane decided to return to the same exercise in six months' time. It would be an interesting measure of development.

The advantage of metaphor is that it allows supervisees to create their own reality and this empowers them. Metaphor can be used to explore work as a whole, or a small aspect of it. For example, the whole practice can be described by a metaphor, or how the practitioner views an individual patient. Lahad (2000) sometimes asks his supervisees to think of their clients as systems:

I ask my supervisee to think about his client or clients, which may be a family or a group, as a mechanism such as the machine or car, or a system or organisation such as a factory or a circus.

It can also be a place such as a central bus station or an airport. When my supervisee chooses the metaphor we explore it, using many questions. (p.63)

FACILITATING A GUIDED VISUALIZATION

In this section we consider guided visualization, used together with relaxation, to help the supervisee uncover hidden insights.

According to the supervisees' previous experience and preferred learning style, they might be pleased or excited by the suggestion of visualization. However, if they are very left-brained, and used to thinking things through, they might feel uncomfortable in a situation where they are encouraged to let go of their self-control and go with the flow. They might express resistance through closed body language or they might say that they find visualization is a waste of time, or that it doesn't work for them.

For others it might cause some anxiety, if they have not done it before. They might feel vulnerable, or uncertain about 'getting it right'. They could feel anxious that visualization will work like some sort of hypnotherapy, where they would be under the power of the supervisor.

We recommend a gentle, undemanding attitude on behalf of the supervisor, especially if you suspect resistance or anxiety. We suggest that you offer this as a try-out that won't take up too much time, and might be fun. You should emphasize that there are no rules, no correct way of doing it and no right or wrong answers.

At the other end of the spectrum, very occasionally some people can be oversensitive to this sort of work, especially if they are very right-brained and intuitive. These are the sort of people who drift off too easily and become spacey. Inviting someone to enter a dream world can sometimes cause problems if they cannot wake up and join the real world again. In 15 years of experience, Jane has only seen this happen twice, and these were after particularly long visualization sessions.

To prevent this happening, we recommend that you make sure the supervisees are fully grounded before you start. Engage the thinking, logical brain for a few minutes by explaining the process. Make sure they are seated with a good connection to the ground, with both feet on the floor, preferably without shoes, or sitting directly on the floor. Have some water, and even a small snack such as crackers available, for anyone who might feel spacey after visualization. The familiar act of eating and drinking rapidly brings anyone back into the physical here-and-now.

The supervisor should always explain what is going to happen before starting, and reassure the supervisees that there are no right or wrong ways of doing it. Then they can ask the supervisees to sit quietly and comfortably with good contact with the floor and their eyes closed. If someone is not happy closing their eyes, they should look at a plain area on the floor or the wall. The supervisor should talk them through the visualization, using a low, gentle voice, with pauses to allow the supervisees' imagination to flow.

All visualization work is best accessed through reducing active thinking and allowing the mind to drift, day-dream, create stories or make pictures. It is usually best to begin with a short relaxation. If the body is relaxed and calm, then the mind has a better chance of being calm as well. The relaxation does not need to take long. For example:

> Sit quietly and feel aware of your feet/body on the floor, and your chair supporting your weight... Allow yourself to relax... Listen to your breathing and any other sounds that are in the room... Take one deeper inhalation and let it out as a sigh... Return to normal breathing... With the next few out-breaths, relax all the little muscles around your face and neck... Sit quietly and enjoy this moment of peace and quiet, etc.

Then the visualization can begin. For example:

> In your imagination, see or feel yourself to be in...

Most people can see pictures in their imagination, but not everyone. So keep your visualization instructions fairly neutral, balanced between seeing, feeling and just being. You don't want your supervisees to feel guilty that they could not see what they were supposed to.

At the end of the visualization, you need to find some words that will bring the supervisees out of the dream world and into the present. Jane uses, 'Allow yourself to gently come back to the present, and, when you are ready, open your eyes.' Be careful not to do any further work until everyone has opened their eyes.

CASE STUDY

A homeopath came to see Jane for supervision on her practice. She had graduated a few years earlier, but now she was finding her full-time job as a school secretary was taking up all her time and she felt unmotivated to do any homeopathy.

Jane wanted to encourage her to self-reflect, in order to find out why she was unmotivated. She started off with a direct approach and asked the homeopath why she thought she was unmotivated. The homeopath was unable to answer. Jane moved to an indirect approach and asked her to write a list of what her ideal practice would look like. The supervisee saw herself doing her homeopathy on Saturdays and evenings. She said she would stop working from home and hire a clinic room. She would see people of all ages, but without too much severe pathology until she had gained more experience. She would get a colleague to locum for her when she went on holiday.

Jane then asked her to do a visualization. After a few minutes of relaxation, she slowly read out her description of the ideal practice, including as many of the homeopath's own words as possible. She asked her to notice her emotions as they came up. When she finished this simple exercise, the homeopath could identify the problem. She said:

> I was quite nervous when we started the visualization, but, as soon as you said I would have a clinic room, I relaxed. I realize now this is what has been holding me back. It feels more professional to go to a clinic room rather than working at home. I get anxious working at home, because I'm alone, and it doesn't feel safe. I'm the sort of person who needs to go to a workplace.

From this realization, the homeopath knew clearly what her first step had to be – to rebuild her practice and her motivation. She needed to find a new clinic room. Jane asked when she would do this, and she took out her diary and pointed to the week when she would have time off work. Jane asked her to make another list, to identify the perfect clinic room she would look for, and they did a positive visualization to consolidate this.

In this case example, visualization was used to explore the emotional background of a fairly straightforward list of characteristics, previously agreed. The emotional content rapidly clarified the whole situation, and the action plan was obvious. Notice how the clinic room had been mentioned from the first, but not identified as the key to the problem until the supervisee was given the opportunity to notice her emotions.

Another visualization that might have had the same outcome would have been to ask the supervisee to work symbolically, as in the first visualization below.

TOPICS FOR GUIDED VISUALIZATION

- *My workplace.* Ask the supervisees to go to their workplace in their imagination, and notice what it looks like, smells like, sounds like, tastes like and what it feels like to touch. In this visualization, the content starts off in the real world but soon moves into a symbolic arena. When asked about the colour of their workplace, the supervisees can find a literal answer, but as the questions progress towards taste and touch the visualization becomes less real and more playful. Facilitating a group doing this exercise, we have heard answers such as, 'My practice sounds like a brass band', 'It feels like Velcro®', 'It tastes like porridge, and I don't like porridge'.

Here are some other visualizations that provide useful insights into the work as a whole.

- *The wise woman or wizard.* Take the supervisees on a short journey during the visualization, starting with a favourite place. Invite them to progress through fields, to a small cottage, where they meet a wise old person who gives them precious words of advice about their work. An alternative ending is that they are given a gift.

- *Lost property.* Ask the supervisees to walk through a small town with shops and cafes, to the lost property office. Instruct them to fill in the appropriate form, and wait while an official goes away and returns with a package. The supervisees find somewhere quiet to open the package and discover what is inside. This is slightly different from the wise person's gift because the idea of lost property holds within it the idea of reconnecting with something from the past.

- *Pandoras box:* Take the supervisees on a journey, from a favourite place, through fields, to a dark wood, to a small cottage, to a small room where they find a box, which they open. Ask them what comes out of the box. When we first started doing these box visualizations, we allowed anything to come out of the box, but this can leave the supervisees with a negative result that needs to be dealt with further. A gentler version that we recommend is that one positive quality as well as a negative one comes out of the box.

- *Allotment:* This begins in spring time when the supervisees are given some unmarked packets of seeds, which they plant on their allotment. Ask them to visualize that it is now summer, and discover what sort of plants have grown. When the visualization has finished, you can help the supervisees appreciate the symbolism of their choice of plants. Unwittingly they will be describing themselves and their journey as they project themselves into the seeds and plants.

- *The Three Bears:* This archetypal children's story is useful to help identify which role your supervisees associate with. You can begin this visualization with a walk through the woods, and finding the cottage. Ask them which bed or seat they find the most comfortable. Once this is established and the supervisees are brought back to the present, you can help explore the symbolic meaning of that choice. We could assume that the position of the father bear represents authority, power or responsibility; the mother bear represents nurture, nourishment or intuition; and the baby bear is associated with having no responsibility and being free to simply play. However, you need to verify with the supervisees what their interpretation of the three roles is, in order for this to be a valuable exercise for them.

Other visualizations are focused on the relationship between practitioner and client, or supervisor and supervisee.

- *Desert island*: This is a visualization that was introduced to us many years ago. You can ask the supervisees to imagine a desert island, creating a landscape of rock or sand or greenery. Then invite them to imagine themselves on the island, where they do some activity. Finally their client or patient arrives. Ask them to visualize the interaction with the other person as well as what they experience emotionally.

- *The mask*: Invite the supervisees to think of their client or patient, and visualize the mask that they might present to the world. Then ask them to look underneath that mask, to discover the inner face of the client. Discoveries like these can add to the practitioner's understanding of the client or patient. It should never be taken as fact, but can inform future work with them.

- *The tunnel*: Ask the supervisees to meet their client, and to set out on a long journey together. As part of this journey, they have to walk through a long, dark tunnel. Get them to visualize what happens.

- *An animal*: In this visualization, you can suggest that the supervisees are walking with a client when the client turns into an animal. Ask them to see if they can identify the animal and to visualize how they interact with it.

At the end of the visualization, ask everyone gently to come back to the present and open their eyes. Allow time for the participants to reconnect with the real world. Some people take longer than others. When everyone has fully opened their eyes and when they have relaxed into their normal body posture, then you can start with the next stage. We recommend that you ask them to take a few minutes to write down the experience in their reflective journal or make a drawing of it. Visualizations can disappear with the rapidity of a dream so, for maximum benefit in supervision, they need to be recorded.

DRAWING THE VISUALIZATION

Drawings done after a visualization can be useful and satisfying for supervisees. This is especially true if you encourage them to let go of any artistic expectations, and just enjoy putting marks on paper. In terms of supervision, a drawing can help consolidate the visualization, or it can reveal new information.

We distinguish our use of drawings from that of art therapy. When you the supervisor view a completed drawing, you should not interpret what you see but rather offer an observation to the supervisees of what you notice. If your description of the drawing does not resonate with them, then they should be free to reject it. This is all part of the process, and you can encourage them to use their acceptance or rejection of your description to help identify their own thoughts.

Silverstone (2009), in *Art Therapy Exercises: Inspirational and Practical Ideas to Stimulate the Imagination*, gives us the advantages of working with drawings:

> To become more integrated, we need to engage both verbal and non-verbal intelligence, both rational and intuitive knowing. Art therapy is one of the creative modes to keep us away from cerebral, verbal, judgemental processes, and in the here-and-now world of imagination, intuition, inspiration. The paradox applies that in thinking less it is possible to know more. (p.16)

She goes on to say:

> Images have very much the mysterious quality of dreams – something we fetch up from within, put out there, hardly knowing, at first, what they are about. We need to bring a kind of reverence, an awe, to work with images. They have an aura of the 'as-yet-unknown', requiring our respect. (p.17)

CASE STUDY

Jane was invited to teach at a college several years ago. Both the venue and the teaching style were new to her. After a couple of months, she wanted to review how she was getting on and what changes she needed to make. She took some quiet time to visualize a metaphor by herself. It came to her that she was standing on a hill, being blown by a brisk wind. She described it in her journal as 'a windy day, exhilarating, gusts of warm air, clouds scudding, patches of blue sky, and the occasional sudden, short, downpour' (see Figure 5.2 on the following page).

Figure 5.2 A girl on a hilltop on a windy day

Extending this into a drawing revealed new information. Jane is standing in the sunshine, with arms raised as if in a dance or in excitement. But the situation is vulnerable, with the wind and the rain, and her feet are not properly on the ground. She went back to her journal again, to examine where she was not fully grounded and what she could do about it. The outcome was that she asked for a meeting with the college principal.

Creative visualization

Creative or positive visualization is a technique of using the imagination to manifest something new that you want in your professional life. It is a type of goal setting, using the power of the imagination to speed up attaining results. Sportsmen and women increasingly use positive visualization, alongside exercise, to increase their performance. The inner game, used by them, focuses on the end result as a way of achieving success. It has been used by patients in hospital to get well. They visualize their healing and surpass their doctor's expectations, walking out of hospital long before others with similar conditions or disabilities.

Doidge (2008), in *The Brain That Changes Itself,* shows the link between imagination and ability by looking at the neurological wiring in the brain. He describes:

> In some cases, the faster you can imagine something, the faster you can do it. Jean Decety of Lyon, France, has done different versions of a simple experiment. When you time how long it takes to imagine writing your name, with your 'good hand', and then actually write it, the times will be similar. When you imagine writing your name with your non-dominant hand, it will take longer both to imagine it and write it… Both mental imagery and actions are thought to be slowed down because they are both products of the same motor programme in the brain. (p.207)

Gawain (1978) wrote in *Creative Visualisation*: 'Form follows idea' (p.19). She develops this idea, saying: 'The idea is like a blueprint; it creates an image of the form, which then magnetizes and guides the physical energy to flow into that form and eventually manifests it on the physical plane' (p.19).

Even without scientific language, Gawain demonstrates how imagination can influence outcomes. In another example from his book, Doidge (2008) writes about Alvaro Pascual-Leone who in the 1990s, while working as part of Harvard Medical School, did a series of experiments that demonstrated people can change their brain anatomy by using the imagination. In one of his experiments, he taught two groups of people a sequence of notes on the piano. One group spent two hours a day for five days, imagining playing the music. The second group actually practised the music on a piano. At the end of the time, both groups were asked to play the sequence and a computer measured the accuracy of their performances. The imagining group were only slightly behind the practising group; and, interestingly, both groups had equal changes in the motor signals to their muscles.

Doidge (2008) also says:

> One reason we can change our brains simply by imagining is that, from a neuroscientific point of view, imagining an act and doing it are not as different as they sound. When people close their eyes and visualize a simple object, such as the letter *a*, the primary visual cortex lights up, just as it would if the subjects

were actually looking at the letter *a*. Brain scans show that in action and imagination many of the same parts of the brain are activated. That is why visualizing can improve performance. (p.203)

Visualizing like this can be used in supervision to make positive changes. For example, someone might be aiming to change their efficiency, time management or interpersonal skills. These changes can be made through visualization, alongside other techniques, such as keeping a positive achievement journal. Visualization can be used to build up confidence or to make learning easier while studying.

Research has proved that we can change our minds and bodies through the power of the imagination and positive visualization. Taking this a step further, authors writing about the law of attraction propose that positive visualization can change the outside world as well. This is different from changing your own inner attitude through visualization; this is aiming to manifest a material change such as an increase in workload or income.

Losier (2007), in his book *Law of Attraction*, says: 'The Law of Attraction may be defined as: *I attract to my life whatever I give my attention, energy, and focus to, whether positive or negative*' (p.7).

He goes on to say that we don't have to deliberately visualize to make this happen. It can happen any time that we are focusing our attention on something through remembering, pretending, daydreaming, or observing our current situation. Remembering focuses on the past, pretending or daydreaming is telling yourself stories about the future, and observing the present can be focusing on a lack or an abundance.

According to the law of attraction, you will create the same pattern in the outside world as you have in your inner world of thoughts. If you are sceptical about this, take a few minutes to think of the number of times it has happened in your own life already. Remember all the times when you have thought about someone and told yourself, 'I must telephone that person' – and they have telephoned you. You can use this in your work. If you think about a particular client, they will then manifest. Both of us have experienced this on a regular basis.

Gawain (1978) says:

Thoughts and feelings have their own magnetic energy which attracts energy of a similar nature. We can see this principle at work, for instance, when we 'accidentally' run into someone we've just been thinking of, or 'happen' to pick up a book which contains exactly the perfect information we need at that moment. (p.18)

A colleague needed a dentist appointment and made a mental note to phone the surgery. Within a few hours, they phoned him to remind him of his appointment the next day. 'I haven't made an appointment yet!' he said, 'But it suits me and I will come.' In fact the receptionist had made a mistake in telephoning him, but the dentist made sure to see him because it was their mistake. He got his appointment just by thinking about it.

These are positive examples, but the same can happen with negative thinking. Have you ever told yourself, 'I feel so stressed out, I am bound to get a headache or a fever,' and it happens. A friend failed her driving test ten times. Every time she booked another test, she told everyone 'I always fail my driving test, it happens every time, I am hopeless at driving.' It was as if she was asking for more failure, and she certainly got what she asked for.

Throughout many years of supervising practitioners, both of us have repeatedly come across supervisees stuck in a negative vicious cycle. These people unconsciously use visualization to hold themselves in an unhappy place. The cycle works something like this: they lack confidence and have doubts about their own abilities for success, which they dwell on. These develop into negative visualizations that produce yet more negative results. Noticing this disappointing result becomes another visualization in itself, reducing success and confidence even more. Any of the methods in this book can be used to turn around this vicious cycle, increasing confidence and visualizing success.

Creative visualization can be done either as a guided visualization, similar to exploratory visualisation, or it can be done through any of the other methods described in this book. In the case of the homeopath earlier, both types of visualization were used. The exploratory visualization led her to realize that she needed to find a clinic room. She was asked to list the characteristics of the ideal clinic room. (Spacious room, window that can open for fresh air, foliage plants and comfortable seats.) This was followed by a creative visualization, in which this list was read back to her, and she was told, 'You deserve this room.'

The first step is always to get supervisees to decide clearly what they want. This is goal setting, and needs to be put into a SMART (Specific, Measurable, Achievable, Realistic and Timed) framework. If the supervisees are logical thinkers, they might want to make two lists: one of what they want and one of what they don't want. The 'don't want list' can be scrapped, or a big red 'X' drawn through it; but it is a useful part of the process and helps identify what the supervisees really want. Once the goal is identified, and put into an achievable time frame, together you and the supervisees can choose the method of positive visualization.

If you want to do a guided visualization, always ask the supervisees' permission first. Begin by asking them to sit comfortably, with their feet firmly planted on the ground, and to close their eyes. If they don't like closing their eyes, they can look at something neutral, such as the floor. Ask them to focus on their breathing for a few minutes to relax before you start to lead them through the visualization. Then slowly read to them the list of what they want, expressing it in positive and encouraging language.

Many of the methods in this book can be used as a visualization tool. Any method will work but it should resonate with the supervisees. The supervisees can create a drawing, build a structure using toys and bricks, which they photograph, write a poem or make their own Angel cards, for example. Ideally the activity should also have an element of fun and positive emotion attached to it. The more imagination and emotion that are put into visualizing, the more effective it will be.

Figure 5.3 shows the drawing done by a supervisee who wanted to extend her client list. She has shown an open door, with herself greeting the new clients. She has surrounded the door with positive words welcoming all the people.

A less prescriptive, and more serendipitous, visualization tool, is using newspaper headlines. We could say this is allowing the universe or the collective unconscious to send the visualization words. As with many visualization techniques, there is an element of play in using this.

Figure 5.3 A person in an open door surrounded by words

The newspaper is scanned for positive headlines, which are cut out and pasted into the reflective journal, glued onto a vision board or simply stuck onto the fridge door. The headlines are carefully selected and edited as necessary. For example, an advertisement might say, 'Live life to the full for longer with xx'. This would be cut down to 'Live life to the full'.

A colleague used to cycle a lot but, after a cartilage injury, stopped cycling and lost his confidence in traffic. He found a newspaper headline that said, 'Get on your bike', stuck it on his noticeboard and thought no more about it. A couple of months later, when visiting a relative, he was offered the opportunity to cycle along a towpath next to the river. It was flat, smooth and there was no traffic, only other cyclists. Cycling during the visit was the last thing he had expected, but it certainly fulfilled the headline visualization. The experience built up his confidence and got him cycling again.

Positive thinking

Everyone is deeply influenced by the people around them during their early years. Parents and carers pass on information with the best of intentions, and children frequently turn what they have learned into a life script. If the message was negative, this can have an impact on their thinking, influencing their attitude and actions. Deeply held beliefs, that you 'can't' or you 'shouldn't' do something, hold many people back. But with awareness and practice, negative thinking can be turned into positive.

We recommend working with the positive, at all times. It is a part of the process of creative visualization and will enhance your work and your mental and emotional well-being. As a supervisor, you can use it yourself. It is worth getting into the habit of monitoring your thinking so that, as negative thoughts arise, you can reframe them into the positive.

Being in the habit of positive thinking does not mean lying to yourself. It is a simple turnaround that eliminates words such as no, can't, don't, haven't, etc. For example, a supervisor who is trying to build up their supervision work can change the thought, 'I don't do enough supervision work. I have only got two or three supervisees' to 'I am available this week if someone wants to ring up for supervision. It would be great to see someone new.'

In this chapter we have introduced the use of metaphor and two types of visualization. All these help access non-verbal intelligence and intuition. Exploratory visualization can help supervisees access some of their hidden thoughts, emotions or attitudes, so that they can understand themselves better. Creative visualization is a goal-setting tool that can help to change attitudes and outcomes.

Chapter 6

Enjoying Limitless Resources

Can you remember a moment when time seemed to slip by as if it did not exist? Perhaps you recall as a child searching for shells on the shore. Each one was so different with their coils, lines and ridges. Some were sharp and some smooth, some were iridescent with mother of pearl. Yet others were pink or grey or many different shades of white and all were mysterious. Perhaps you found a big one that you placed to your ear and you heard the sound of the sea. As you turned the shell over to look at the other side, the sand ran through your fingers. Time evaporated. As supervisor and supervisee, we may have had this or a similar experience and know what enticing resources these simple objects can be.

In this chapter we focus on the myriad of creative resources that you can draw on and use effectively in supervision. These include pens and coloured paper, pictures of people, toy money, Angel cards, objets trouvés, stones, shells and buttons.

Both of us have worked in a university for many years, teaching reflective practice and practitioner development to CAM (Complementary and Alternative Medicine) therapists. In this setting, we have both developed a facilitative style of teaching that encourages experiential work and enables students to learn through their own discoveries. This has meant reframing many of the lessons so that students are active rather than passive, working with experiential tasks and then discussing, self-reflecting or writing about what they have learned.

Experiential learning can take place in the classroom, in workshops, supervision groups or with a one-to-one supervisee. We frequently use props or resources to support this work. These are the physical and practical aids to teaching or supervision that bring in another dimension and stimulate the imagination. Throughout this book, we interchange the terms 'props' and 'resources'.

The more obvious resources are the students themselves and visual aids such as pens and paper, whiteboard, PowerPoint and a projector. Beyond these there are a whole range of other props and resources that are effective and stimulating for students or supervisees. Some of these take a little time to collect or set up, but it is time well spent. Once they are part of the supervisor's prop basket, they can be used in many different ways. As Minton (1997) says in *Teaching Skills in Further and Adult Education*:

> The major purpose of visual aids is to create a change of focus. They help to create attention...
>
> Since we experience 70 per cent of what we learn by using sight, visual images and presentation are very powerful aids to learning. They are usually more effective than sound alone. Most people's seeing skills are much more highly developed than their listening skills. (p.85)

Minton is here referring to visual aids and resources being used in teaching. We suggest that using resources facilitates both the learning of new material and self-reflection on any piece of work that has been done. Stimulating resources encourage supervisees or students to view the work from a different angle. They start to work differently, accessing their right brain which taps into their intuition, non-verbal thinking and their emotions. The supervisees can engage with these skills, temporarily becoming lost in the process of creativity. On completion of the task, they can sit back and observe with fresh eyes what they have created. They can then engage with it intellectually. This process of working from the right side of the brain, pausing for a moment, and then working from the left side of the brain, can greatly enhance self-reflection.

Props can be used to represent people, issues, values, dilemmas or goals. Some props or resources represent an archetype. This can happen when working with toys and figurines, when we ascribe archetypal qualities to them from mythology, such as the wisdom of an owl or the loyalty of a dog (see Chapter 4). This can also happen when working with photographs, because we become attracted to the qualities we see there, such as friendliness, intelligence, hard work, relaxation or fitness. Other props have their own intrinsic value – for example, a stone can be heavy or dark coloured – and can represent anything we choose. We project our own meaning onto these objects.

It is our experience that, as soon as a collection of interesting resources is brought out, the atmosphere in the room changes. There is a feeling of excitement, anticipation and playfulness. It is as if the boundaries have suddenly shifted from an intellectual, working environment to something more relaxed.

Lists, charts and diagrams

We begin with a resource that at first sight appears to be without value. Paper is one of the most versatile and easily obtainable resources. It can be used for constructions, crumpled, folded, sprayed, torn, used as a template or made into papier maché. Its applications are various. Having a variety of different coloured papers, and coloured pens or pencils, allows for a whole range of writing or drawing exercises. Narrative and poetry are long-lasting if they are written down. Visualizations would probably be forgotten if they were not written down or drawn. Anything created on paper during the supervision session can be taken home and fastened into the reflective journal afterwards.

Pens and paper can be used for lists, diagrams and charts as well, which are satisfying for left-brained, logical, thinking people. Anything can be put into a quick and effective list. For example, supervisees who are considering finding another job, could make a list of what they need in order to be happy in their next job, such as congenial colleagues, flexible working hours or in-house training. Someone else, wanting help with designing a webpage, could list what they like or don't like about other websites they have visited, such as the font size, the amount of information, the quality or content of the photos, and so on. For many people it is useful to write a second list, expressing what they do not want. This can help clarify what they do want, and when it is completed the rejected list can be torn up, thrown away or a big red 'X' can be drawn through it.

A development of writing a list is making a mind map or spidergram, which are more dynamic and more visual. When running workshops to teach supervision skills, we ask everyone to make a mind map of their support network. This is an effective way of demonstrating how far spread a support group can be, and reminding them that they should not depend on their supervisees for emotional support. Similarly, supervisees can make a mind map to remind them not to depend emotionally on their students, clients or patients.

Ask the supervisees to put themselves at the centre of the mind map, and connect this with lines to everything that supports them. This might include, for example, their own supervisor, colleagues, friends, family, their faith or spirituality, books, pets or plants, music, hobbies, sports or their computer. In fact anything can be added that gives this person mental, emotional or physical nourishment. Further detail can be added to the quality of the lines of the map. Notice if the individual items are firmly connected to the central figure, or are they wavering, at a distance or disconnected (see Figure 6.1).

My support network

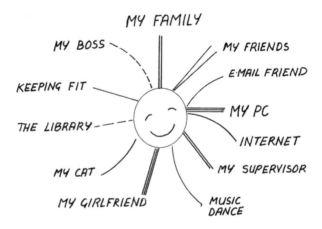

Figure 6.1 Mind map with face in the centre

Tree diagrams, Venn diagrams, flow charts, pie charts and bar charts can all be used to represent issues that come up in supervision. Caroline sometimes asks supervisees to draw their own story as a timeline. They often find this clarifies all the issues for them. To set this up, she provides the supervisees with a large sheet of paper and asks them to use it in any way that they want to show their timeline with significant professional and personal events. The majority of people do this in a linear way but occasionally you will find that people become creative with the task. One of Caroline's supervisees cut up the sheet of paper, made a book out of it and presented their life in book form.

We have used pie charts very effectively with supervisees who have problems with time management. To do this, ask the supervisees to think about how they fill a normal week. Then ask them to create a pie chart showing how their time is divided up between work, study, friends, family, household chores, hobbies and relaxation, for example. They might need a pencil and eraser to plot down the initial lines. Once the pie chart has been completed, the supervisees often express surprise or regret at the division of time. The next step is to ask them to draw a new pie chart, showing their ideal division of time.

Sometimes supervisees have negative beliefs about their artistic skills and refuse to do a drawing as part of supervision. If you ask them to do a diagram, they feel much more secure. We suggest that you don't distinguish between diagrams and drawings, recognizing them both as creative acts and useful visual aids.

Photos and picture postcards

This resource comprises a large collection of photographs of people. They can be collected up from postcards or magazines. Postcards, depicting cartoons, famous people or artworks can be bought from holiday resorts, museums and art galleries. Photos can also be cut from magazines and glued onto plain pieces of card. (You can buy A4 or A5 index cards from stationery shops or you can recycle suitable pieces of card.)

Choose photos of various people to represent different archetypes. They can be young or old, male or female, calm or emotional, eccentric or traditional. To provide you with the richest resource, they should ideally represent the full diversity of the human condition, with people of different religions, ethnicity, colour, age, sexuality and culture. For example, a set of cards could include a princess, a crying baby, a running woman, a wise-looking old man, a couple who are cuddling, a punk teenager, a doctor in a white coat, a threatening bully, a glamorous film star, a sculpture with a wooden face, a king from the 15th century, a dancing girl, a man with a dog, a cartoon character, a woman with a skin condition, a man in old-fashioned army uniform, someone wearing a mask, a woman holding dollar bills or a man crying. The list could go on. The collection should have somewhere between 20 and 100 cards.

Once you have collected these cards, they can be used in a variety of different ways. For example, they can be used to help supervisees examine their self-identity as a person or focus on one aspect of their life, such as their professional role. Choosing cards can raise the questions: How do you see yourself and how do you want to be seen? What do you aspire to? We start with an exercise for looking at how the supervisees see themselves.

WORKING WITH PICTURE CARDS

Explain to your supervisees that you have a range of cards that you're going to spread out on the table or floor. Ask them to look them over carefully and choose a limited number of them (we suggest about four) that summarize how they see themselves. The chosen cards should be placed where both of you can see them. Both supervisor and supervisee will have a turn in discussing what they see. With this exercise, it could be either of you who speaks first. The supervisees are probably impatient to explain what they have chosen, but it might be to their advantage to listen to you first.

As the supervisor, you should talk about your observations of the choice of cards. As usual, feedback should be clear, owned, balanced and specific. As well as noticing the choice of person within the picture, you can also talk about the colour and focus of the photography. For example:

> The postcard of the running man shows energy and speed, but it is a wet and miserable day, and he is running through puddles. He looks very fit and purposeful, but personally I wouldn't enjoy

running in the rain. The overall colour is grey. As one of your choices my reaction is that it is great to be so energetic and busy, but I am wondering if you are missing out on fun.

This comment would be balanced by examining the other three postcards, which might indeed show more fun.

If this exercise is being done in a group, you could ask another group member to give the feedback. If the group is small, numbering three or four, then everyone can receive feedback from each member of the group.

CASE STUDY

A student practitioner asked Jane to provide supervision for his graduation cases. As they worked together, Jane felt dissatisfied with the student's work, because the case taking was too superficial and brief. She spent several sessions with the student, working through the case line by line, trying to explain to him why he should have asked different questions, or encouraged the patient to talk more deeply. The student felt strongly that he didn't want to push his patients. Jane felt that the student would be unable to make effective prescriptions unless he found out a lot more about his patient. They reached an impasse.

Jane asked the student to return for another session, and she carefully prepared a pile of picture postcards that all had some relationship to the caring professions. She invited the student to choose four cards to represent how he saw himself as a practitioner and the student chose eight, refusing to narrow his focus. Jane asked the student to explain his choices of cards and then picked out the two most extreme of the eight pictures: these were the 'loving dad with children' and the 'surgeon standing next to his tools ready for an operation'.

Jane encouraged the student to discuss these two pictures in depth, questioning and challenging his beliefs and values. The student wanted to be the benevolent father to his patients, but liked the professionalism of the surgeon. Gradually through discussion, he accepted that the surgeon's role is to cut with a knife, in a controlled way, in order to heal. The student began to realize that sometimes it is necessary, much like the surgeon, to go deeper. This session opened up some new ideas for the student, but further work needed to be done to consolidate change.

After the session, Jane reflected on the student's choice of eight cards rather than four. She realized that this was yet another example of his personal preference to look at things from a broad perspective rather than a deep one. The experience of being persuaded to narrow his focus onto two cards and discuss them in depth was probably not comfortable for him. However, experiencing this for himself, outside the consulting room, would encourage him to try it again. She made a note to herself to refer to it in the next supervision session.

A different way of using the picture cards is to use them as a goal-setting tool. You can ask the supervisees to think about how they would like to see themselves in six months or a year's time. In order to focus the mind, invite them to choose four to six cards from your collection.

A slight variation on goal setting is to use the cards to consider the values that the supervisee has or would like to have. By values we mean the moral, ethical or emotional beliefs that influence people's attitudes. In the later section on Angel cards, the supervisee is asked to work with named values, seeing them written and rewriting them. If the same piece of work is done with picture postcards, the values might not be named, but they are intuitively felt and identified when choosing the pictures.

If the cards are being used with a group, the facilitator needs to make sure there is a large enough selection. If two people want the same card, they can decide to share it one after the other, or they might decide that neither should have it, and both can discuss their feelings at lacking this quality.

Angel cards

Angel cards can be bought in packs or they can be handmade. There should be at least 24 of them, with one or two words written on each, expressing a positive value. Examples of values are appreciation, balance, benevolence, calmness, commitment, compassion, co-operation, energy, enthusiasm, flexibility, honesty, humour, integrity, listening, love, mindfulness, openness, peace, practicality, tolerance, trust or wisdom.

These cards can be useful in helping supervisees to define themselves in relation to their work, their colleagues and clients. Values underpin many interactions and using these cards heightens an awareness of them. When working with Angel cards, we like to provide our supervisees with a stack of blank business cards (calling cards) of various colours and some felt-tipped pens so that they can make their own cards. We encourage them to keep these and use them as an aide memoire.

CASE STUDY

Jane was running a supervision group for practitioners, and unusually everyone came with the same issue: how to build up their practice. Jane writes:

Two of the practitioners had moved house within the last year, and had deliberately allowed their practice to run down, but now they felt ready to expand again. The third practitioner was feeling the effects of the recession. She knew that she should be doing mail-outs and telephone calls, but wanted to see if there was anything subliminal that she had missed.

As this group had worked together trustingly for a long time, I decided to start in the deep end and asked them to make a list of their fears and negative fantasies about expanding their practice. I was interested to observe that all three of them lacked confidence. When I questioned them, it appeared this lack of confidence was fairly recent and was not around when they first began as practitioners. I encouraged them to discuss this and reach some conclusions. Some of the issues were around perfectionism, and there was relief in the room when someone stated clearly that no practitioner or doctor ever gets 100 per cent success rate in their cases.

Following this discussion I asked them to write another list, this time stating their positive qualities as practitioners – for example, their listening skills, their relationship with the patient, or their experience with a certain group of people, such as children or the elderly. This second list led to further discussion.

The practitioners who had moved house needed to discuss the practicalities of setting up a clinic room within the new space. The rigour of the supervision session was starting to drift and I could see that the third practitioner was becoming bored. We were coming towards the end of the session so I suggested that we finish with Angel cards. The third practitioner became quite excited and requested that we place the cards on the floor face down, so that they could be picked out at random. Everyone agreed, so I laid the cards out and recommended that everyone had a minute or two of silence before choosing their cards. They all felt they received excellent guidance through the cards, in particular the third practitioner who had originally asked for something subliminal.

As all the cards had positive qualities on them, I felt it was completely safe to let the practitioners choose at random. Any card they chose would have had an interesting message for them. They could have chosen the cards with the face up, but this would have been working with qualities that they knew they needed. Choosing the cards without seeing the value written on them allowed a less conscious and more intuitive process to happen.

Caroline has often used Angel cards in ending group sessions. She will place the cards in a hat or box, or she might improvise by tying a scarf up to make a container for the cards. Then she will pass this round and let everyone choose a card. The message on the card becomes a symbolic gift from the group, and invites further reflection. A slightly different version is when every member of the group writes a value on a blank card that is put in a container and then passed around. Sometimes people pick out the value that they put in. Maybe on an unconscious level this was what they needed all along. Maybe they needed, symbolically, to be able to give something to themselves.

Objets trouvés

Jane was facilitating a creative supervision workshop at the Homeopathic Supervision Conference held by the Society of Homeopaths in Sheffield in 2004. She brought a sack full of toy animals and some bricks, and planned to ask the participants to think of a boundary situation; they were to make a small constellation that they could share with a partner. Working out the logistics of doing this with a large group, she realized that she had not brought enough bricks with her. The night before the workshop, she hastily collected and washed out a couple of dozen portion-sized plastic milk pots.

Another time, meeting at a colleague's house to do supervision, Jane wanted to work with toys and props. Her colleague looked around and rapidly piled up a sparkly Christmas decoration, three carved wooden ducks, a miniature teddy bear, a shell, an empty spice jar, a pen lid, a clothes peg and a carved stone cat.

The point of these two stories is that a whole range of props can be provided at a moment's notice to use for supervision. An interesting selection of items can be collected for regular use. For example, seashells, coloured plastic bottle tops, pine cones, cotton reels, marbles, key rings, colourful erasers, pencil sharpeners, Christmas decorations and souvenirs. It creates more interest if your collection can include a variety of textures, weights, shapes, sizes, materials, reflective qualities and so on. Those who like working with their hands can make interesting shapes out of coloured polymer clay. A bowl of highly polished river stones, together with a few polished semi-precious stones and crystals invites the supervisee to touch. The same effect is felt with a bowl of brightly coloured buttons or beads.

Other props can even be discovered in handbags and briefcases, as Proctor (2000) suggests in *Group Supervision: A Guide to Creative Practice*:

> When supervisors in training are asked to brainstorm every possible creative exercise they have used or could imagine (with clients or supervisees) the list is endless. Many have never thought of using familiar devices in supervision context. Supervision is helped by a conducive location – spacious, relatively comfortable, with potential for using, for example, paper, colour, clay, soft toys as props; better still if it is soundproofed or isolated from other users. Even in cramped and cramping circumstances, there are props to hand. The contents of handbags and briefcases; clothing and jewellery; all can be used as projection objects – as metaphors or to elicit comparisons. Also pebbles or buttons can

be used to map or 'stand for' different aspects of client/councillor relationships. (p.184)

A supervision session using objets trouvés should start with an explanation of what is going to happen and a negotiation with the supervisees. All elements of the case, issue or incident can be represented by an object. Every person involved can be represented, as well as inanimate objects. In one constellation, the client's diary was represented by a large cotton reel with endless thread, because it figured so strongly in the interview. In another constellation, where the practitioner was concerned about the amount of recreational drugs being taken, the drugs were represented by a weighty, dark stone. A colleague was doing a constellation in which she put a couple of cushions on the floor, and balanced the objects on top.

As with many other methods in this book, you should allow the supervisees to work in silence, accessing their intuitive knowledge of the situation while you observe them. When they sit back, relax or sigh, their body language usually shows that they have completed what they need to do, and are ready to discuss what they have made. It is better that they receive some feedback from the supervisor before trying to explain the situation. Your feedback as supervisor should always be clear, balanced, fair and owned. You can refer to your own intuitive observations, using phrases such as 'I feel', 'I notice', 'My impression is', 'From where I am sitting it looks like'. This can develop into a dialogue between you.

Each item is judged by its intrinsic characteristics. The stone is large or small, shiny or rough, dull in colour or bright. The marble will not stand where it is placed but tends to roll out of position. The plastic bottle top is either a tiny plinth or a container. The seashell is white and chalky, but if you turn it over there is glossy pink inside. They all become actors in the drama that is represented. Your observations of these characteristics can help the supervisees understand their issues in more depth.

Stepping stones

Goal setting comes up regularly in supervision. Frequently the supervisees can identify something they would like to do, or have, but they can be indefinite about what exactly it means for them, or how they will achieve it. They might wish or hope that it will come about, but find it difficult to come up with an action plan. As supervisor, you can help them clarify whether this is what they really want (writing a list might be useful) and set them on a more active path where they can achieve their ambition. There are several different tools and skills that you could use – for example, positive visualization, making a drawing or writing a narrative.

One technique that we have used successfully in workshops is that of stepping stones. As usual with all the methods in this book, you should negotiate with the supervisees before doing this piece of work. Once supervisees have clarified the goal they really want, they can write this in large letters on a coloured piece of paper, preferably A4 sized. From this they have to work backwards, using another six pieces of coloured paper to represent the different stages along the journey. You can encourage this process by asking them what they will have to do to achieve their goal, what order these steps will be in and when they plan to do each one. Once they have written on all seven pieces of paper, these should be placed along the floor, with the goal at the most distant point. The supervisees then physically stand on each stepping stone in turn, saying what they intend to do as they progress towards their goal.

Stepping stones works particularly well in a group, where all participants witness each other's journey over the stepping stones. This is a physical journey as well as a mental one, and its benefits are enhanced by the encouragement of the rest of the group who act as cheerleaders.

Caroline had a supervisee who placed her stepping stones all over the room including on chairs. She then had to work out a way of getting from one stone to another and realized how hard she was making her journey, both physically and in reality. This allowed her to revisit her goals and make the path simpler. It is always worth noticing in the feedback the trajectory that is taken. Is it a circular journey or a linear one, and does it flow easily?

The stepping stones process involves both rational left brain and the intuitive, emotional right brain, so it is a particularly useful exercise. In deciding the steps, supervisees need to make every stage a SMART goal in itself – that is, Specific, Measurable, Achievable,

Realistic and Timed. This is logical and sensible, but only half the story. Walking the stepping stones, and making a conscious choice to feel excited and positive about achieving the goal, involves the emotions, which in turn increases its efficacy. When the whole self is involved in an exercise like this, rather than just the intellectual part, it becomes more powerful. Walking through the stepping stones embodies the experience and helps to make it a reality that can be achieved.

CASE STUDY

An academic decided on the following steps, working towards her goal of publishing an article:

- Create regular dedicated time in diary: January.
- Confer with peers for support: January.
- Check other publications in my field: February.
- De-clutter office and PC: February.
- Research article: February–March.
- Write article and submit: by 2 April.
- GOAL: publication in peer journal: June.

She made these into stepping stones, deciding to put some stones side by side because they applied to the same month. She had fun jumping from the double stones to the single stones like a game of hopscotch. In our feedback on her work, we observed that she had made a staircase. Everything was leading towards her goal (see Figure 6.2).

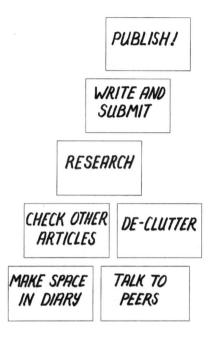

Figure 6.2 Seven steps to get published

Making money

A prop that brings out excitement is money – perhaps because of its many different associations such as affluence, poverty, greed, consumerism, reward, freedom, comfort or spending. Some self-employed people have a problem with charging money, either from shyness or from moral doubts. Others who are employed often find it hard to ask for pay rises. We have found a two-pronged approach the most effective to help address this problem.

The first step is to ask supervisees to reflect on their family's attitudes towards money. Family messages about money can be imprinted very deeply from an early age, creating strong beliefs about the acceptable levels of affluence or poverty, as well as whether it is the norm to talk about money at all. If this work was being done one-to-one, probably a short guided visualization would help the supervisee to let go of these attitudes. Sharing these messages in a group reveals how much of a hold the outdated beliefs of previous generations have, and frequently a group discussion is enough to let go of the past. In one group workshop that we ran, we created a long list of these beliefs, such as, 'money doesn't grow on trees', 'you have to work hard to save money', 'your dad earns it and your mum spends it', 'you should always do some charity work', and 'it's bad manners to talk about money'.

The second step is to offer everyone bundles of paper money and ask them to do a role-play where they spend it or receive it. This works in a group or one-to-one. Together with role-play partners they act out the last ten minutes of a session together. The role-play partners should act as if they are reflecting on a service they have just received (such as a tutorial, workshop, massage, acupuncture session, supervision or something else). They give feedback in terms of strengths or weaknesses, offer a tip or attempt to negotiate a reduction in fees. The supervisees should maintain their integrity, answer any criticisms calmly and demand the correct fee. In one workshop, a participant burst into tears when she was offered a tip. Exploring this, she realized she had many deeply held beliefs that she was not worthy of receiving a reasonable fee, and certainly did not deserve a tip. This reflection was a great insight for her and enabled her to start the process of change.

There are many sources of paper money, so ready currency does not need to be used. Play money does very well, and a little colour can be added with the leftover notes from holidays abroad. Some of our most impressive 'money' comes from £25 vouchers, decorated and scrolled like English pound notes, and distributed as advertising in order to persuade people to buy certain products.

Develop props of your own

Using props, resources or visual aids encourages flexibility. Sometimes one technique can be replaced by another. When Caroline joined a new supervision group, each member was asked to bring a significant object with them to use to introduce themselves. Interestingly, some of the people forgot to bring something, but there were some ingenious solutions to this. One of these came from someone who had meant to bring the bells that she used for her Indian dancing classes. When she realized that she had forgotten them, she quickly drew a picture of them while she described the dancing. Learning to improvise is as important as being well prepared.

As you become familiar with these techniques, we hope that you will develop new ones. To begin with, you might feel you need to be well prepared for each session, and you may want to practise the techniques as we have described them. As time goes on, you can use the group or supervisee to help in generating other methods of creative supervision, using the props already collected or designing new ones. We suggest that you keep yourself open to feedback from your supervisees about the techniques you have tried out with them. Creative supervision can be ever-changing and ever-developing, according to the needs of the supervisee or group.

Chapter 7

Creating Narratives

Imagine for a moment that you are looking at a tree from your window. What do you notice? Perhaps its shape, its size or its colour. What would happen if you opened the window and saw it more closely? What would happen if you went out and touched it? What else might you see? As you near it you might notice the pattern on the bark, the veins on its leaves, a tiny fly or ladybird on the underside of the leaf. This process of deepening your understanding of the tree is similar to the process that occurs when you create narrative and explore it.

In previous chapters, we have focused on effective forms of supervision that can be done without necessarily going into the minutiae of a supervisee's 'story'. Here we explore ways in which the story itself and the process of telling and receiving it can be central to the supervisory process. We show how different techniques using spoken or written narrative can be usefully applied to the supervisory and reflective process. In addition we look at how you can make creative use of poetry, drama, narrative and retelling stories.

By 'story', we mean the narrative supervisees construct for themselves about an event or an issue. It is their own personal experience and the way in which they choose to tell it will be unique to them as well as being culturally determined. Narrative forms work well on a one-to-one basis and can also be used in a group setting.

Zeldin (1998), in his book *Conversation: How Talk Can Change Your Life*, says of conversation:

> Conversation is a meeting of minds with different memories and habits. When minds meet, they don't just exchange facts: they transform them, reshape them, draw different implications from

them, engage in new trains of thought. Conversation doesn't just reshuffle the cards: it creates new cards. (p.9)

Through the supervisory process, a particular type of conversation is had in which the supervisees' stories are retold. The process of being listened to, challenged and having the stories explored makes it possible for the supervisees to reconstruct them for themselves and to gain a different perspective on them. As Garro and Mattingly (2000) state in *Narrative and the Cultural Construction of Illness and Healing*:

> Narratives never simply mirror lived experience or an ideational cosmos, nor is a story a clear window through which the world, or some chunk of it, may be seen. Telling a story, enacting one, or listening to one is a constructive process, grounded in a specific cultural setting, interaction and history. Text, context, and meaning are intertwined. (p.20)

Supervisees arrive with an issue that seems stuck, unresolved or only partially resolved. They tell the story from their own perspective. Whichever creative form of supervisory process is engaged in, whether using a narrative approach or receiving words, songs or poetry by way of feedback, the supervisees will be enabled to reflect in or on action and co-create a new reality through the supervisory process. In the case of enacting a story, the supervisees will go through a felt bodily process of aligning themselves to their subject as well as finding a new perspective.

Retelling stories using poetry and song

We have found that poetry and song are effective ways of reframing an experience in order to understand it. Poetry often uses symbolic and metaphorical language that can bring with it multiple interpretations that further enrich understanding. This technique can be used one-to-one, but really comes into its own when used with a group.

We recommend that, as with other creative techniques, it is best to use poetry once a good working relationship has been formed. If these techniques are new to supervisees and used early on in a relationship, you might find that they become self-conscious and maybe more resistant.

By way of introducing this way of working, we sometimes find it helpful to start a session by reading out a story or poem, or playing a song or piece of music. The rationale behind doing this is that it reminds the group of the shape, sound, rhythm and structure of songs, music and poems, and stimulates creative thinking.

CASE STUDY

Caroline sometimes opens a session by reading out a poem. In her poem below the rhythm is built up through the repetition.

I wanted to take it home with me

I wanted to take it home with me
the smell of burning wood in the cold, clear air.
the sumac splashed red across the grey rock faces,
the melting sun meeting with the moon.
I wanted to take it home with me.

I wanted to take it home with me
the walnuts gnarled at my feet,
the yellow finger leaves where I never knew walnuts to be,
the lizard out for a second in the sun, scurries between the rocks,
the pink winter roses hang heavy by the reddened tomato plants.
I wanted to take it all home with me.

I wanted to take it all home with me
the quiet cold, clear air,
the grey mountain around,
the little village folded in the rocks
lives buried within my mind.

We have noticed many different responses to these opening stimuli. They will range from emotional reactions to cerebral ones that focus on the form, content or structure of the poem or song. Whatever the response, most people will have one. We always recommend you to respect and honour the variety.

Groups suitable for this sort of work are those in which all the individuals have a common aim, such as supervision, training or self-development. Everyone has to provide some material that they wish to work with. For example, practitioners might want to discuss a case in order to understand the client more fully. Students might want to look at an aspect of their work such as their learning styles, or anxiety around assignments. Team leaders might want to reflect on their leadership style and what impact this has on their team.

To begin this way of working, we suggest that you invite the group to sit in a circle, so that everyone can see each other's faces. In keeping with all the other techniques in this book, we recommend that you do a mini-contracting session, explaining what will happen before you begin. Allow the group to decide between themselves who will be the first to present an issue. This person becomes the storyteller, and is invited to present the issue in five to ten minutes.

Ask the group members to listen to the story and observe whatever is striking for them about it. (They can take notes if that is helpful.) Once the story has been told, they will be given five to ten minutes for writing their response to it either as a poem or a song. When everyone has completed their contribution, they will all read their work back to the storyteller by way of feedback.

Remind them that this is not about perfecting an art form; rather, it is about catching the flavour of the story and the particular aspect that has resonated with each member of the group. It is about highlighting something that you have understood or felt and handing it back to the storyteller in a new and different form.

The advantage of giving it back to the storyteller in a new format is that the essence of the story becomes distilled in its journey. It began as a mixture of fact and feeling in the mind of the storyteller. Then it became a verbal presentation to the group, and finally it is given back to the storyteller in a transmuted form. This act of transformation gives it an added potency. It can allow the storyteller to see a new perspective as well as sometimes confirming things that they sensed but could not name themselves.

After all the songs and poems have been read out, you should ask the storyteller if they would like to reflect further on the issue, and they are given the opportunity for discussion; ten minutes would be enough time. At the end of the session, we recommend that the storyteller should be given all the poems and songs in written form to take away with them. These can then be used by them for further reflection in their reflective journal (see Chapter 9).

CASE STUDY

One of the most interesting sessions we had using this technique happened in a workshop we were running. A practitioner had presented a case where she felt uncomfortable with her client, and the group were asked to write their responses as poems or songs. One of the group members wrote a haiku where she used minimal words to sum up the essence of the client.

Cold slithering
Through the grass
Here now

This was powerful for the original storyteller as it highlighted for her the unsavoury nature of the person she was dealing with. When she was in the presence of the client, she had repressed her feelings in order to remain professional. Receiving the poem enabled her to honour her feelings and plan her future relationship with the client. In the same session another participant handed her a poem, which she had sung to a rap tune while another gave her rhyming couplets.

TELLING THE STORY FROM DIFFERENT PERSPECTIVES

A different version of this exercise can also be done with a group. In this version, the facilitator listens to the storyteller's issue and asks the other members of the group to particularly notice any personae that are mentioned during the presentation. When the presenter has finished, the facilitator invites the group to write the story from the viewpoint of someone else in the story. These can then be read back to the presenter, allowing them to consider and find new perspectives.

Acting out a group issue

Within organizations there can sometimes be departmental or inter-departmental issues, struggles or misunderstandings that could benefit from being looked at and processed. Talking about the issues may help if the whole group can get together. Later in this chapter we demonstrate how using a reflecting team can help to facilitate this. If there is an opportunity for a staff away day, a good alternative to talking is allowing the staff members to literally act it out.

Acting a play is a group activity in which everyone represents and enacts someone else or something else. The focus should be the main issue that is bothering the group members. They can use furniture to set the scene and dressing-up clothes to get into their chosen parts. The facilitator needs to negotiate the amount of time necessary for preparing and acting the play, as well as time for getting feedback on it and having some discussion afterwards. A carefully planned and rehearsed play might take up to an hour in preparation. On the other hand, telling the participants that they only have 15 minutes in which to prepare, demands that they trust each other and be spontaneous. Shortness of time can often sharpen the mind and lead to focused and revealing work.

If you are able to organize this in advance, create a box of props. This can be anything you choose from false moustaches to walking sticks, top hats, paint brushes, clothes, lengths of fabric, costume jewellery or Wellington boots. A good mix of objects and clothes helps stimulate the imagination. If it is an impromptu session, props can be found among the participants' outdoor clothing, and paper can be used to make hats, fans or masks.

Through the process of enactment and play, the participants will have an opportunity to air their grievances. Often when these plays become comical or satirical, they highlight more clearly the areas that need most attention. The use of humour and laughter can take the emotive charge out of a potentially difficult situation and at the same time they can illuminate what needs to happen. Landy (2003), in his chapter 'Drama Therapy with Adults' in Schaefer's book *Play Therapy with Adults* suggests that: 'When the play is applied to a therapeutic process, as it is in drama therapy, a conscious purpose arises – to offer a commentary on, or corrective of, everyday life, thereby gaining a greater sense of control' (p.31).

Debriefing afterwards allows time for reflection and discussion both on the creative process itself as well as reviewing the original issue. Engaging in a joint venture like a performance is an excellent way of team building, and can in itself improve working relationships. It broadens an understanding of individual members and new aspects of them will be revealed.

CASE STUDY

Caroline helped to develop supervision groups for clinicians at the university where she works. The university provides degrees in a range of complementary therapies. Part of the students' training consisted of taking a compulsory core module on reflective practice and facilitation skills. This increased their ability to reflect on their work and the therapeutic relationship. Some of their clinical supervisors had not had this opportunity and this disparity could sometimes create conflict in clinic. Supervision groups for clinicians were set up to provide them with a supportive, safe space for bringing their issues and to encourage the habit of self-reflection.

The supervisors involved in the project decided to present their findings at the Homeopathic Supervision Conference in Sheffield in 2004. Instead of writing a paper, they wrote a play entitled *Three Acts of Many*. It was a reflective piece looking at the whole process of getting the supervision groups up and running.

The play was presented by three of the university supervisors, reading from prepared scripts and asking for audience participation. At times members of the audience were asked to step into the shoes of the clinical supervisors and act as if they were them.

The play highlighted some of the main difficulties involved with this project. To begin with, some of the clinicians appeared wary of the groups and questioned whether there was a hidden management agenda. There were misunderstandings about what supervision was. There were discussions about whether the supervision groups should be interdisciplinary, paralleling the student study groups. Everyone had to make personal decisions about commitment, and what issues they felt were safe and useful to bring into the supervision groups.

At the end of the play, members of the audience were divided into small groups and asked to give feedback on some of the aspects of the difficulties seen in this process. Finally, they filled in a questionnaire, which they handed in.

The play represented something of the experience of setting up supervision groups within the university setting. However, by using the audience, who had not been involved with the organization at all, new issues were identified and reflected back to the actors. This was an invaluable process that led to further reflection and a refinement of working within these groups.

The audience had a deeper understanding of the problems involved with this project, having taken part experientially. The short timeslot for the entire presentation meant that a careful balance had to be made between the play being acted on stage, audience participation in the role of clinical supervisors and the final feedback.

Co-creating the story

Launer (2002), in his book *Narrative-based Primary Care: A Practical Guide*, has developed a particular type of supervision, which he calls 'conversations inviting change'. He pioneered this narrative way of working with GPs and more recently with clinical supervisors and teachers. We have experimented in using this method in supervision groups. The principles apply well to supervision in any setting because they are generic.

This process is creative in a different way from some of the other techniques in this book. Its particular form of creativity relates to reframing 'stuck' stories that supervisees bring. This helps them re-story their dilemma.

Narrative supervision engages supervisees in a particular type of conversation about their issue or dilemma. Some of the key ideas come originally from family therapy, using techniques of eliciting multiple views on reality and of using a reflecting team. Unlike other techniques in this book there is no emphasis on the unconscious at all: this method is in the here and now of the conscious world.

Key to this kind of conversation is an exploration in which the supervisor remains curious about all aspects of what is being said. The supervisor asks only open questions and works with the supervisees to explore their issue while steering clear of giving advice. The emphasis is on facilitating the supervisees to come up with their own answers.

If advice is being sought during the conversation, this might be given at the end of the supervision. One strategy for avoiding advice giving is to encourage the supervisees to give themselves advice by asking, 'If I were to give you advice, what would be useful to you?' That forces them to think more deeply for themselves. Another strategy would be to ask them what advice someone else might give them.

The narrative approach to supervision allows the story to be co-created and re-created by the supervisor and supervisee and by the group if this is a group setting. It is a model that is ostensibly non-hierarchical. Through the re-creation of the story, a wider perspective is opened up, providing opportunities for the supervisees to reflect on why they were stuck within a smaller story, and often clarifying the way forward. This method can be used one-to-one or in a group.

Launer (2002) says: 'Narrative ideas offer a conceptual framework for understanding all the different discourses... Narrative ideas can also provide practitioners with the skills to help patients and colleagues alike to question, re-evaluate and change their own narrative' (p.2).

Launer proposes that the key elements of the process are hypothesis, circularity and neutrality. The hypothesis is the idea that develops for the supervisor in regard to the supervisee's issue; through exploration and questioning, this hypothesis gets revised and a new one emerges. Circularity means asking open questions to bring in other perspectives on the issue – for example, 'Who else is there around you and how may they view it?', 'What other reason could you give for their behaviour?' or 'What would they say?'

This form of supervision draws out many different perspectives from the supervisees, which create a rich tapestry of meaning. The supervisor remains in a neutral place. Neutrality in this model means not engaging with any one of the views but simply eliciting them. At different stages of the discussion, the supervisor will check out with the supervisees where they are in their exploration and whether they feel that they are on track.

There is always the caveat with this style of supervision that the issue may not be totally resolved in the session but may end up evolving into another conversation.

John Launer highlights what he calls the 'seven Cs' of this supervisory process. These seven Cs echo much of good supervisory practice but perhaps have a different emphasis from other models of supervision. The seven Cs are:

- conversation
- curiosity
- context
- complexity
- caution or challenge
- care
- co-creation.

We would add that as in any supervisory process there are other issues that have to be borne in mind, such as confidentiality and respect for everyone within the group; support, which ideally should accompany challenge; creativity; awareness of verbal and non-verbal cues and sensitive timing of questioning. The length of a narrative supervision can vary and, as this way of working becomes more familiar, the timing may be reduced.

SETTING UP THE GROUP

We have used this technique in peer groups and when facilitating supervision groups. To begin working this way, we suggest you ask everyone to sit in a circle and talk briefly about a current issue that preferably has not already been reflected on. Each person should tell the group about the issue in the form of a headline or soundbite that encapsulates it and gives a hint of the areas causing concern. Some examples of this might be 'a case of pushing the boundary', 'I feel bullied', 'How do I get a response from my boss?', 'One of my students keeps texting in class' and 'My line manager doesn't listen to me.' You should ask the group to choose which of these topics they would like to begin with, and then agree timings.

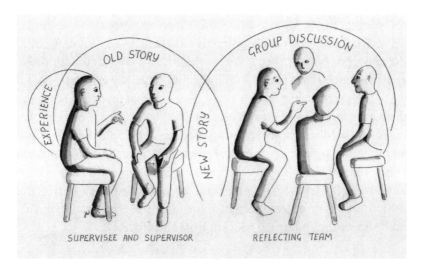

Figure 7.1 Supervisor, supervisee and reflecting team

The supervisor faces the supervisee at a distance that is comfortable for them both, and the rest of the group, the reflecting team, sit in a circle slightly away from them but within earshot. The reflecting team may consist of two to five people. If you are teaching this method to a group, then you could take the role of supervisor to model the technique. Once you have demonstrated it, a volunteer from the group could work as supervisor with you as mentor. The mentor sits beside the designated supervisor and either of them can interrupt the process, freezing the conversation, if help is needed. Making a 'T' shape with the hands asking for time-out is a useful way of doing this.

While the supervisor and supervisee are talking, the reflecting team are silently listening and absorbing what is going on. From time to time, the supervisor can freeze the action and ask the reflecting team to have a conversation among themselves. They are not commenting on the process or solving the problem but having a conversation about what has been discussed. What they have heard may also have generated new lines of thought. Sometimes being in this space without consciously thinking can produce the most remarkable insights. The reflecting team act almost like the collective unconscious, picking up unspoken ideas and naming them. We see the role of the reflecting team as resembling that of a Greek chorus (see Figure 7.1).

The supervisor and supervisees listen to this conversation without responding to it. After a while the supervisor stops the reflecting team. The supervisees are then asked whether there is anything from the conversation that they have overheard that resonated with them, and which they now want to take further. This is particularly useful when the supervisor is feeling stuck. This external input can move the dialogue on and bring a fresh perspective.

Finally, feedback is given by the reflecting team, then the supervisor, and then the supervisee. Feedback should be focused on the process rather than the content of the session. Sometimes the supervision flows so well that the reflecting team are not called upon during the session, but their observations at the end of the conversation enable both supervisor and group to learn from the process.

ASKING OPEN QUESTIONS

It can take practice to acquire the phrasing of apt open questions, in the manner recommended for supervising narrative conversations. But once you have learned the technique, it is a tool that you can use in any other area of supervision.

It works best if you pay close attention to the exact words used by a supervisee so that you both come to understand the meaning and context of what is being said.

You can ask short, open questions to allow exploration, and you should encourage the supervisee to stay with the same issue and look at it from many different perspectives – for example, considering it from the viewpoint of another protagonist. One of the differences with this form of questioning is that you always follow the thoughts of the supervisee in the present and do not return to previous topics. Your role is not to advise or guide the supervisee in any way, unless there is a professional or ethical issue. Your role is to enable the supervisee to explore the issue from many different perspectives.

The use of open questions can help to reframe or review an issue. 'What' and 'how' questions generally help to develop and expand the meaning of what is happening. For example, 'What might your line manager think of your actions?' or 'How else might you look at this outcome?' A 'why' question might elicit a 'because' answer rather than facilitating reflection.

CASE STUDY

Caroline brought an issue to a supervision group where everyone took turns at being supervisor. The headline was 'Patient not seen in a year demanding I send out an instant prescription'. The acting supervisor listened attentively following her narrative, exploring how Caroline viewed the situation primarily as an ethical dilemma. She wanted to act professionally and have a proper consultation with the patient because she had not seen the patient for a year. However, the patient would not come and just wanted a prescription, so Caroline was torn because she wanted to help with the patient's discomfort.

A turning point in the narrative came when the supervisor asked her how she thought the patient viewed her. She realized that in the past she had played a very supportive and almost parental role to this patient who was new to this country and had small children. She had been attentive and perhaps, on reflection, over-involved in helping this family. Perhaps she had been viewed as a surrogate parent. This realization allowed her to see that she did not want to continue in this role, and that her initial response of it being unethical to send out the remedy without further discussion had been right. She came up with an action plan of writing and explaining to the patient that she did not send out repeat prescriptions after this length of time without either a full telephone or personal consultation.

Thus it was possible for Caroline, with the help of the supervisor, to imagine how the patient might have been viewing her. In so doing she was able to change her own behaviour and feel happy with her decision. She was also able to create a story viewed from the patient's perspective rather than her own. This in turn helped her to change her own behaviour, leading to the creation of a different relationship with the patient.

The questions from the supervisor were so pertinent that the reflecting group did not have to be used very much. After Caroline had had her realization about her previously parental role with the patient, the group members were asked to reflect on what they had heard. They offered a few insights, which were further explored. At the end of the session, they gave feedback on the process, helping both the supervisor and Caroline reflect on what had worked well in the supervision. From Caroline's perspective, the short, simple questions had efficiently and effectively helped her to reframe the story from the patient's point of view.

REFLECTING TEAMS IN ORGANIZATIONS

Reflecting teams can be used in exploring organizational change such as a change of direction for a company, a departmental merger or the implementation of new working practices. Taking this into supervision, we work with two circles. One consists of an interviewer or facilitator and a group, which is the active, working group; and the other is the listening, reflecting group. The reflecting group does not have eye contact with the active group and just listens to what is being said. The participants are in a cooler space, out of the heat of the main discussion. The facilitator can instruct them to listen out for certain threads of the story, such as what might be lost by the changes proposed, what might be gained, what could be given or any assumptions that are being made. They could also be asked to focus on their reactions to what they hear.

In your role as facilitator, you should explore what the changes mean for the members of the active group. Your role is to help them all to identify their individual stories. At a suitable point, you should freeze the discussion within the active group and turn to the reflecting team. You can ask them questions based on the specific areas they had agreed to observe, or you can ask them to have a discussion based on what they have heard. Alternatively, you can be more specific and ask for three questions that the active group would like answers to from the reflecting group.

Using narrative as reflection in action

Working with the narrative in this way demands that you accept that someone's story is not fixed or set in stone. It is part of a process, ever influenced by the retelling of it by the storyteller, and by the impact of the listener, both verbally and non-verbally.

The same ideas can be used to work in a one-to-one way with a client or supervisee. As usual with the techniques in this book, you need to check first with the other person that this is all right.

CASE STUDY

Caroline has used this technique in the consulting room, working directly with the patient, rather than discussing the patient with a supervisor. In this instance, the patient asked her what she would do in a particular situation. The patient had had an operation to replace a bodily part, and the replacement part was noisy. At times it felt noisier than others and it really bothered the patient. Caroline consulted quickly with the inner voices of her own reflecting team and came up with some thoughts. She asked her patient if it was all right to explore this creatively and playfully for five minutes, using a different technique.

Caroline didn't want to give advice, but used the narrative technique to explore a few ideas. She imagined herself as a solo reflecting voice, with many different thoughts and ideas, bubbling off with the patient listening in. Caroline decided to be playful. She knew that the patient was musical and began wondering out loud what tune the part might be playing and how she could engage with it. The patient was a little dismissive and but, after a few minutes of thought, she said, 'That has given me an idea. I could use it as a monitor of my emotions and if I am angry I could use it to think about the people who might have angered me. I think I shall develop this idea myself.'

The idea of imagining something outside the situation and playing with the story seemed to change something. Even though the patient did not take up the suggestion itself, it triggered her to reformulate the problem and make creative use of it. Thus using play and conjecture was helpful to her.

Here is another example where Caroline used conversation and imagination, working directly with a patient.

CASE STUDY

This patient had recently had a flare-up of a chronic condition. When the flare-up started three weeks earlier, the patient was hardly able to walk and was constantly tired and unable to work. Caroline prescribed for him and advised him to rest. Three weeks later he declared himself 95 per cent better but he still wanted something tiny fixed. Caroline asked him to consider what part this tiny annoyance might be playing in his healing. There was silence and then the patient laughed and said, 'I get it, it is stopping me from going swimming and getting back in the fast track. That's clever.'

Through this conversation he was able to acknowledge that he was beginning to get impatient. More than this, he had the important insight that he still needed to keep the energy he had and not start to use it all up. He recognized that he could be in control of his own healing if he listened to his body. By asking him what the final symptom was achieving in the overall healing, Caroline enabled the symptom to have its own voice.

Reflection does not always stem from an issue, dilemma or critical incident but may arise spontaneously. Sometimes an object or some words can trigger reflection. Interesting insights could be gained through exploring and reviewing the stimulating object or words. Meaning may be built up through multiple views of the same thing. It can be seen to be made from the personal as well as social constructions that we have for objects and words.

CASE STUDY

'Everyone tells their own story. But it's a tale which at best will become someone else's story.' These were the words painted on a wooden trolley that was part of a mixed-media installation made by Professor Hans Stofer and shown at Collect (Saatchi Gallery, London, May 2009). It was entitled 'Off my trolley'. The artist had laid out paint brushes, cigarette butts, necklaces and other objects like notebooks on the three levels of the trolley. There was a 'log book' attached to one side of the trolley and on another side of it were words to the effect that art had helped keep him sane.

Caroline experienced multi-levels of meaning from engaging with this work. It allowed her to question the notion of sanity. The quotation may have had an intimate relationship with the trolley itself, which contained notebooks that might have been personal jottings, notes or reflections on a state of mind. Perhaps it might have been a reference to how mental health patients may not be heard or may not feel that they are heard. It showed her how using an object can conjure up a multitude of connections both symbolic and highly personal. The trolley seemed literally to become the vehicle of sanity, holding within it the artefacts that helped the artist keep a foothold in reality. At the same time, there was the idea of the trolley as an institutionalized piece of furniture, in transit between patients, bringing food and drugs. Beyond this, the trolley may have had a personal meaning for the artist at the time of making the object.

Caroline decided to share the above quotation, without showing an image of the work, with some colleagues and found that they each had their own version of what the words meant. One thought it was about connection while another thought it was about how a story gets changed in the telling and no longer belongs to the teller – it gets transmuted into a story that belongs to someone else. Perhaps this is also true when we narrate our stories in supervision.

The spoken word is potent but appeals more to supervisees who use auditory skills as their primary way of communicating. Working with a group will mean that some people are working in a way that may not best suit their learning style. However, making this explicit and allowing for experimentation can sometimes lead people to make remarkable insights about themselves. As with other techniques in this book, the use of narratives, drama, poetry, song and stories can be extended as far as the imagination goes, and the group itself can be used to generate new ideas for their use.

Chapter 8

Using People as Props

We would like you to bring to mind three different types of sculpture: the etiolated figures of an artist like Giacometti, a group sculpture such as Rodin's *Burghers of Calais* and a reclining figure of a mother and child by Henry Moore. When you do this, you might notice that you project an emotion or a story into these figures. Perhaps you feel a poignancy in Giacometti's lone spindly figure; you might be drawn to the scale of Rodin's piece and the way in which the people are weighed down and connected by heavy chains; in the case of Moore, maybe it is the blankness of the mother's face that draws you in, or her relationship with the child. Whatever your reaction is, you will have one to the sculpture as a body in space. So too in supervision, we can engage with the body on a visceral and a physical level to give us powerful information about ourselves and the people we work with.

In this chapter, we look at different ways of using supervisees as physical bodies both in relation to space and also as a resource. This is in contrast to previous chapters where we have recommended using props. Props are useful because they are external to the self and, once identified or placed in a certain way, can be used by supervisees to reflect on. This allows them to become the observers of their own work. Using people as resources can be done in the same way; if there is a large enough group, they can be used as actors under the direction of the facilitator or supervisee. Examples of this are group sculpts and family constellations. In the case of triads, the placing of the supervisee, supervisor and observer in relation to each other is relevant.

People can also be used as resources for their observations or supervision skills, where they can actively contribute to the supervision process. Using techniques such as triads, the supervisee can take a turn at becoming the supervisor. In these cases, your role becomes more like a meta-supervisor, meta-observer or facilitator.

Yet another use of people as resources is with role-play. This can be used to re-view the past in order to understand it better – for example, re-creating the non-verbal body language of a client (someone that you have met). Role-play can also be used as preparation or a rehearsal for something that will happen in the future.

Choosing your chair

In some cases the size of the room will limit the seating arrangements. But most rooms allow some flexibility, and as a supervisor you can either set up the furniture before the supervisee or group arrives, or change it according to the needs of the participants. The way in which the chairs are arranged in a room will play a part in determining the relationship of the participants both to each other and to you. You can choose whether to sit with the group, or separate yourself by sitting further away or behind a desk. Your seating position and your body language will all become part of the non-verbal information you are communicating to the group or supervisee. For example, a supervisor who chooses to sit behind a desk or table might be variously perceived by some supervisees as wanting power, being powerful or as shielding themselves.

When people come into a room for the first time, in order to do a workshop, supervision session or seminar, they generally choose their chair very carefully. If they recognize other people, they might want the safety of sitting close to a friend or colleague. If all participants are strangers to each other, on the whole they will choose the chair that does not encroach on someone else's space, but at the same time one that is not too distant. Once chosen, the chair becomes the assigned territory and safe space for the occupant, and they return to it throughout the session. Possessions are put around or underneath it, as markers of occupancy.

Most or all of the techniques discussed in this chapter involve the supervisees or participants moving their chairs, or temporarily using a different chair. This immediately takes them physically away from their comfort zone, and you will probably notice that some group members may be resistant to moving their chairs. When teaching, we have encouraged students to take up the entire room when doing small group work, in order to get out of earshot of the other groups. But in the early sessions some of the participants find it difficult to even change the angle of their chair from its original position. Carrying it to a different part of the room is almost impossible for them at first, until they have settled in and observed other people doing it. If you keep a sensitive awareness of the group's needs in relation to territory then you can decide when is the right time to challenge them.

Role-play

Role-play can be used for two different purposes in supervision. It can be used to re-create what has happened in order to understand it further, or it can be used as a rehearsal for something that hasn't happened yet. In the first instance, the re-enactment becomes an embodied experience; in the second, it is imaginative acting. Its use can be empowering and can increase confidence.

CASE STUDY

Caroline had a supervisee who wanted to expand her teaching work. She had managed to get two interviews lined up at higher education institutions, and she felt apprehensive. Caroline asked her to try and identify her fears. Once this had been done, she asked her whether she would be willing to engage in a role-play. Caroline chose to sit behind the desk to role-play the interviewer. They played through many different scenarios, from discussing her CV to asking specific questions about her teaching skills and her personal life. By the end, the supervisee had made an action plan: to check her wardrobe and find appropriate clothes, to write down and memorize key points about her teaching experience to date and to take copies of her published articles with her to her interview.

Through the role-play she had started to conquer her fears and prepare herself for the interview.

TWO-CHAIR WORK

An empty chair can be used to symbolically represent an absent person. The supervisee may wish to rehearse or review their relationship with that person; or a group might want to include an absent colleague. In these cases, participants can talk to the chair as if the absent person were sitting there.

A more dynamic version of this, which originated in Gestalt therapy, is to have two chairs that supervisees can alternate between. They can be themselves when in one chair, and role-play the other person when seated in the opposite chair. This gives them an appreciation of what it's like to be the other person. We can never fully imagine or understand what another person is thinking. However, sitting in the other person's seat, and feeling intuitively their non-verbal and verbal responses can activate a deeper understanding of them. It also provides the opportunity for the supervisees to see or feel how the absent person views them. This can give them a heightened appreciation of the dynamic. Once they have done this, they can reflect on this new information.

This technique can be used in one-to-one work. When used in group supervision, it is useful to get the rest of the group to observe the supervisee. As they enact and embody the absent person, the supervisee will take on certain postures and gestures. When the observers give feedback on this, it can give the supervisee doing the two-chair work even more insight into the absent person.

At the end of the two-chair work, we recommend that you encourage the person who has worked to come out of role. There are several ways of doing this. Moving back to the original chair will help. Another way is to brush the body with the hands as if to physically dust off the mantle of the other person. Yet another way is to say, 'I am' and add your name, then 'I am not', adding the name of the client. Doing this will help the supervisees regain their own bodily stance again and become themselves.

MIME THE FIRST FIVE MINUTES

If the supervisee wants to discuss a client or patient, a very good strategy is to work with role-play. This is much faster than verbally describing the absent person, while still bringing the person into the room. The aim is to re-create the body language and non-verbal communication, using eye contact, tone of voice, gestures and facial expressions. It does not matter if the original words have been forgotten.

The supervisor or a group member works with the supervisees who act or mime their client. Suggest that they can either act the first five minutes of meeting the client, including greeting them at the door, or any key five minutes that they would like to explore. Ask them to take a few minutes to remember and reflect on their client before they begin. When they act, it can be with or without words. After the five minutes of acting has been completed, everyone should come out of role. Then you or the observers, if there are any, can give feedback on what it was like to be in the presence of this enacted person.

ROLE-PLAY WITHOUT EYE CONTACT

Another useful role-play is that of a telephone call. This should be done without eye contact, sitting side-by-side or back-to-back. This sort of role-play is usually used as a rehearsal, to practise what has been planned out previously.

CASE STUDY

A homeopath came to see Jane for regular, long-term supervision. She appeared very confident and talked about her cases in a very positive way. After two or three supervision sessions, she said she had an issue about phone enquiries. She was self-employed and was her own receptionist. She said that when a new patient phoned up to make enquiries about homeopathy, she went pink, stammered, talked awkwardly and felt like a child. Jane suggested that she spent five minutes writing down what she would really like to say and then they would do some role-play. Jane asked her to face away from her and she would act as a patient phoning up and making enquiries. After this they discussed what happened, and between them they came up with a further list of suggestions:

- to deepen her voice slightly, to sound more confident

- to involve the patient in a conversation by asking them what they already know about homeopathy

- to research into choosing patient-friendly words

- to notice the level of understanding of the patient, adjust her vocabulary accordingly and avoid using jargon.

Finally they did a second role-play so that she could practice all the new ideas.

In November 2007 we ran a workshop on creative supervision at the Confer 'Power of Touch' Conference in London. As an experiment, we asked the participants to work in pairs, sitting back-to-back, while one of them talked about a clinical experience. The people who were listening found that they could not hear so well, because physically the voice was being projected in the opposite direction and they missed out on picking up visual clues. But on the other hand, they received a lot of non-verbal information through the skin and muscles of their back, feeling the other people breathe, sigh, vibrate as they talked and move as they used hand gestures. We observed that, when one pathway of understanding is closed down, another one takes over. Here sensory perception has become heightened as visual and auditory cues have been lessened.

Triads

Triads are a structured way of working in a group of three people, each taking it in turns to supervise each other. There are three roles – the storyteller, the active listener and the observer – and three designated chairs that they rotate around. The active listener is the supervisor, and the storyteller is the supervisee. The observer learns through watching the other pair and gives them balanced, constructive feedback when they have finished.

Triads provide experiential learning. They are a valuable technique for use in group learning or group supervision, because they involve all the participants. Everyone has a defined role, which creates extra focus. Allowing a short time limit of 15 minutes per role seems to focus the work, and remarkable progress can be made in this time. It creates an intensity that means many issues can be reflected on and resolved. This intensity may lead to feelings of vulnerability and exposure, which can be minimized through clear contracting and tight organization. Triads are often used in training, in supervision groups and in peer groups.

Depending on how close they sit to each other, the supervisor and supervisee will feel more or less at ease. Similarly the observer can sit at different distances from the supervisor and supervisee and get a different perspective on the process that is occurring. When facilitating a triad, your role becomes more like a meta-supervisor, meta-observer or facilitator.

Before you start, make sure that everyone understands the ground rules for this exercise. Everyone should be clear about their roles, no one should speak out of turn and everyone should keep to time.

Ryan (2004, p.157), in *Vital Practice*, has created a list of functions of triad practice, which includes:

- to practise moving in and out of role, encouraging empathy with each position

- to practise the awareness of the nature of formal space and time – clarifying intention, making and maintaining working relationship, contracting, working with time limitation, boundaries, flexibility, focus and effective use of the space

- to practise being present

- to practise the art of active listening, getting alongside and minimal intervention.

SETTING UP TRIADS

In order to set up a triad, place two chairs at a comfortable distance facing each other, not too near and not too far. These are for the active listener and the storyteller. The third chair is for the observer, and should be placed so that this person can have a good view of the other two people. The active listener and storyteller have ten minutes to work together, including the storyteller's presentation of the issue.

It is easiest if the observer acts as timekeeper, and quietly tells everyone when there is one minute left, so that they can finish off. A useful way of doing this without intruding on the process is to form the letter 'T' with your hands when there is a minute left to go. Once everyone has finished, the observer gives feedback to the active listener only, so that the listener can learn from working within that role. In effect, the storyteller has already had supervision, and now it is the turn of the active listener to have it. The observer should not give feedback to the storyteller. However, the group supervisor may want to ask the storyteller at the end of the session how the storyteller's understanding might have changed as a result of this supervision.

On completing this feedback, all the participants leave their chair and rotate to take a new chair and a new role. They proceed until everyone has had a turn in each chair. Having a dedicated chair for each role makes it much easier to de-role after each session.

If there are four people, the triad can work with two observers. One observer sits in the usual place, and the other one sits further away, observing the other three. The more distant observer might not be able to hear every word, and has to be more perceptive of the non-verbal signals. Second observers, in the 'cooler' space, can also tune in more to their own emotional and bodily responses to the triad work. Their response when fed back may well give useful information on what is happening in the dilemma being addressed.

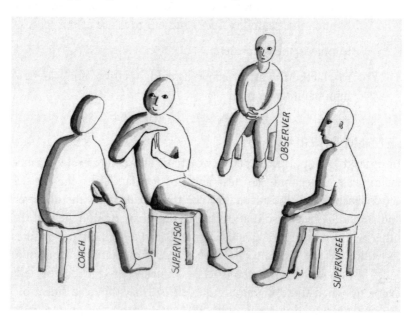

Figure 8.1 Coach, supervisor, observer and supervisee

TRIADS WITH EXTRA HELP

A variation of the triad, if the active listener is lacking in confidence or knowledge, is to ask a colleague to act as mentor or personal coach. You could also take this role. The coach sits close to the active listener, and remains silent. Either of them can call time-out, making the 'T' shape with both hands. They can discuss strategies and possible questions that the active listener could use. The coach only works with the active listener, and does not become involved with talking to the storyteller. When the active listener is prepared and ready to start supervising the storyteller again, the coach becomes silent (see Figure 8.1).

TRIAD WITH SUPPORTER AND CHALLENGER

We developed this extended triad, while working with groups, in order to encourage the group members to use a wider range of feedback with each other. We recommend that all feedback should include both support and challenge. But sometimes group members who have not done this before can find it difficult, so we use this exercise to clearly differentiate between the two. The advantage of this working format is that it liberates group members to be really honest with each other. The disadvantage is that it could potentially overwhelm the supervisee, so therefore it is best done within clear boundaries and a prescribed structure.

In this exercise, the storyteller is flanked by two extra people and faces a supervisor–facilitator. We recommend that you take time to get this positioning right. The two extra people will take the roles of supporter and challenger, and need to sit beside the storyteller, not in front. If the supporter, challenger and supervisor–facilitator sat in a row in front of the storyteller, it could feel confrontational (like a board interview for them) and might be overwhelming. The arrangement comes from the idea of having a devil sitting on one shoulder, and an angel on the other. Viewed another way, it is like having two externalized sub-personalities. Other members of the group can sit as observers.

Sometimes the storyteller craves encouragement, and really appreciates the words of comfort from the supporter. But in our experience, on many occasions, it is the words of the challenger that really make an impact. There might be a moment of shock or laughter, but then the storyteller will want to engage with the words and reflect on them.

You should take the role of supervisor–facilitator, and you should begin by explaining what will happen before you start. Let the two flanking people decide who will take the role of supporter or challenger. Then you can invite the storyteller to talk and, politely at a suitable point, to stop and listen, while the supporter and challenger have their say. The supporter acts as a best friend, giving reassurance, comfort, appreciation or admiration. The challenger should be direct and forthright, saying what needs to be said with no holds barred.

You should prevent any discussion occurring between supporter, challenger and supervisee. As facilitator, you should invite the storyteller to simply overhear what is being said. The supporter and challenger are then asked to sit silently, while you continue supervision with the storyteller again. Ask the storyteller to choose what they want to work with after overhearing the comments from the two aides.

Group sculpt

This works best with a large group, and can be fun and entertaining, as well as very enlightening. It is literally a large human sculpture or tableau, created out of the group, for the purpose of understanding a situation more clearly. Invite the supervisee or storyteller to present the issue to the group in five minutes. Once the issue has been clarified, the supervisee is asked to use all the other participants to create a living sculpture. The other people are placed, like tailor's dummies, into the positions that best illustrate the issue.

CASE STUDY

While studying supervision skills, Jane was part of a group of 20 or 25. One of the participants presented an issue about his consulting room, which he felt was too dark. There was a large tree outside the window. He started the sculpt with a small rectangle of people to represent walls of the clinic, and someone was placed as the door. He included people to represent the desk, the bookcase, the filing cabinet and several chairs. Then he asked someone to act as the tree outside the window. Finally he and his client went into the room. The client said, spontaneously, 'I'm suffocating, I can't breathe, I want to get out of here.'

This physical demonstration of a clinic room enabled the supervisee to see and to feel the atmosphere of the room. It was not just the tree outside the window – it was the overcrowding of the small room that was the problem.

After everyone had come out of role, the storyteller was asked if this had helped him crystallize an action plan. He said he would like to look at clearing out some of the clutter in his room.

Another use for this would be within a corporate situation in which there are proposals for change. The best way of approaching this would be to have half the group making the sculpt and the other half observing what they see and commenting on it. The use of an outside facilitator is strongly recommended in this situation to ensure that an unbiased observer role is maintained.

Family constellations

This technique is very similar to that of the group sculpt, but can include more acting and speech. It can be used to explore complex situations that include several different people – for example, a family situation, a patient who visits several different practitioners, or a student who is divided between home life and studying.

Choose one member of the group to be the storyteller and ask this person to give a brief outline of the story. Get the storyteller to nominate colleagues from the group to represent each person from the story. Sometimes this is done by the storyteller placing two hands on the shoulders of a colleague and saying, 'You are...'

Ask the storyteller to physically move each colleague, both individually and in relationship to each other until a tableau or action scene has been established that best represents the case as the storyteller sees it. The storyteller can ask the players to act. Once the positions have been established, the storyteller can ask the players what it feels like to be that person. As the supervisor, you could ask the storyteller to notice the physical relationships of the players as well as how they look. You might suggest to the storyteller that you add your own observations.

CASE STUDY

Caroline took a case to group supervision. She was puzzled by the lack of progress in this particular case of a teenager. She decided to ask the group to help her enact a family constellation.

Caroline asked the teenager to lie down and the mother to lie close to her. She placed the father with his back to them. The mother was almost melting into the child.

On standing back from this and getting a distance, Caroline was shaken by the intensity of the relationship between the mother and child and the seeming lack of relationship between the father and the other two. The facilitator encouraged the actors to speak from the voices of their parts and the child said, 'I cannot get better. If I do, my mother will leave me.' The father said, 'There is no room for me here.' The mother said, 'I don't want my husband here.'

This was a powerful constellation and brought insight into the case for Caroline. She understood that there was a trade-off for the teenager in not getting better. All the players were encouraged to de-role and come back to the group as themselves.

The group hand clap

Our final techniques that involve people as resources are fast and dynamic. Their pace is the opposite of the quiet and contemplative sculpts and constellations, and they work best with a large group of participants.

The hand clap is an exercise that can be used as a warm-up, or a team-building task. It is dynamic and energetic, and demands that the whole team work in harmony. Everyone needs to be aware of everyone else, and to work together to create a collective rhythm.

CASE STUDY

Caroline was working with a group, and wanted to provide some restorative time for the participants after a busy morning. She writes:

I challenged the group to send a hand clap around the room in the fastest possible time. I started with a brainstorming session. This raised the question of whether they had to go all the way round the circle or whether it would be quicker to do two hemispheres of sound at the same time. The consensus was this did not count as a circle. The group started to experiment with how near or far they should stand from each other, and whether they should start with their hands apart. They discovered that standing further away from each other was more helpful as they could see each other better and they would know when to clap. They discussed whether they would need a timekeeper to identify the shortest time for the hand clap but decided that practice was the best way to speed up. Then someone decided that they needed a rhythm to have a beat and someone started tapping their foot. This got faster and faster as they were clapping and laughing.

It was hilarious and energizing and wonderful for the team esprit. The group also became very competitive with itself. As well as team building this exercise also encouraged the group to reflect in action. As they implemented each suggestion from the team, they observed its effectiveness and adjusted until they had the most effective system.

The two-minute line dance

This is a fast, adrenaline-fuelled exercise in which everyone takes it in turn to talk for two minutes. It works well within a group or workshop situation. The exercise can be used in a variety of different ways, such as a warm-up, a close-down at the end of the session, a rehearsal of specific skills or an advertising pitch. It can be used to introduce everyone to everyone else, or it can be used for everyone to talk about their work. We have also seen it used for a group to appreciate something about each other at the end of a period of working together.

The more shy members of the group may find this exercise challenging. They may hesitate and find it difficult to choose words when they first talk. But if they continually repeat the same task with new partners, they become more fluent and more confident.

The two-minute line dance works best with a group of ten or more. You should arrange the group members into lines facing each other, either standing or sitting. You will need to explain the task carefully before they start the exercise. They are given two minutes to talk to the person in front of them and another two minutes to listen, in the manner of speed dating. You will be timekeeper and, after two minutes, you should bang a gong or shout out loudly that it is time to change. One line of people remains seated or standing still. The other line moves a couple of steps so that each person is now facing a new partner, with the spare person circling round to join the beginning of the line again. It is like a dance, and continues until they have all returned to their original partners.

Using people as resources

Using people as resources can bring insights into a wide range of issues and dilemmas. Here the body itself at times becomes the vehicle for understanding. Its relationship to space and to other bodies becomes the focus, as can the sense of embodiment itself.

Some of the methods we have described involve the supervisee or group in the process of supervision itself, training them in team work and increasing their self-reflective skills. Other methods encourage a sensory experience of someone else, which may lead to an increase in compassion and understanding.

Chapter 9

Developing an Inner Supervisor

Historically the diary, as in the case of *Pepys's Diary*, has been used as a creative tool for recording events. It has also been used as a confessional, like in *Bridget Jones's Diary* where Bridget writes candidly to her diary as if talking to a friend about her difficulties in meeting the right man and all her disappointments. She bares her raw emotions to the diary. Then there is *The Diary of Anne Frank*, which is both a useful historical record of the Second World War seen from the perspective of a teenage Jewish girl in hiding, but is also a confessional in relation to her growing awareness of her womanhood. The professional working journal becomes a historical documentation of your working life but also bears witness to the process that you undergo in reflecting on it. It becomes a self supervisory tool for reflection.

The focus of this chapter is on ways in which you can supervise yourself. There are times when a supervisor is not available, either short term between sessions or more long term. At other times you might wish to prepare before going to supervision, or reflect after the session in order to deepen your understanding. Supervising yourself through self-reflection can have its limitations and demands honesty, self-disclosure and a good balance between acknowledging your strengths and weaknesses. The other option, when there is a lack of supervision available, is to form a peer group. Working with your peers necessitates careful teamwork, good feedback skills and self-reflection.

Professional self-reflection after the event is different from the everyday run of thoughts that goes on in most people's heads all of the time. At its best it takes place in dedicated time, in which you engage specifically in exploring aspects of your work, in order to enhance and improve it. The benefit will be for you and for those you work with. It is a form of continuous professional development, distinct and apart from increasing your learning through reading books or attending lectures and seminars. Self-reflection is the process of exploring your actions, motivations, attitudes and values within your professional and inter-professional relationships, in order to understand yourself and your work better, and implement changes if necessary.

The Johari window (see Chapter 5, p.68) demonstrates that there are some areas that we know completely about ourselves, some areas that we know about but choose to hide from other people, some areas that other people can see but we cannot, and some areas that are completely hidden. The aim of self-reflection is to open up some of our blind spots. These are contained within the areas that other people can see but we cannot, and the completely hidden area.

Having said that, there are limitations to how much you can open up your own blind spots by yourself. You can begin the process but, sooner or later, you will have to engage with someone who can act as an external supervisor. Such a person is in a better position to be objective and to challenge you so that you can open up more of your blind areas.

The reflective journal

Frequently the very process of expressing your thoughts means that they become more defined, and provide the opportunity for change. Talking with a supervisor or writing your reflections on a paper or screen journal takes your thoughts out of your head and into the outside world. The beauty of working with a journal is that you are creating a resource you can return to. Using any concrete form in which to express self-reflections, such as writing or drawing, allows today's thoughts to be reviewed again in the future. It is through reviewing your journal that patterns may reveal themselves that were not obvious as you were writing. Moon (2004), in *A Handbook of*

Reflective and Experiential Learning. Theory and Practice, writes about this secondary learning:

> The content of 'reflective writing' is not a direct mirror of what happens in the head, but it is a representation of the process within the chosen medium – in this case, writing. The representation of reflection in the form of writing is likely to differ from that represented in other ways such as speech or in a drawing. In making a representation of personal reflection, we shape and model the content of our reflection in different ways and learn also from the process itself. In other words, there is secondary learning. (p.80)

According to Moon, reflective writing is a particular kind of writing that goes beyond mere description, and for some people develops through several stages. The first step is often simply a descriptive record. As the process evolves, you may start to incorporate basic reflective questions about what happened. The next step would include a focused description of the event, an analysis and an exploration of why you may have behaved in certain ways.

As the ability to write reflectively develops, you might use a hypothesis about why things happened the way they did; you may view the situation from other perspectives; and you may explore your own learning from the original issue. Deeply reflective writing includes self-questioning and an ability to stand back from the situation and view multiple perspectives. The final stage is the development of the internal supervisor bringing an ability to stand outside yourself and view the situation dispassionately; being able to allow for uncertainties; and being able to review deeply held beliefs and attitudes.

Moon (2004) gives the interesting example of four different accounts of the same incident; this shows how reflective writing can develop from the purely descriptive to the analytical. The final stage is being able to stand back from the situation and acknowledge the part the reflector played in the incident.

There are many ways of using the reflective journal. Among our colleagues are those who write every day, once a week or only when necessary. There are those who write by hand, and those who always use the computer. Some people like narrative, while others prefer bullet points. Most people write about past events, but others make notes for themselves for ideas to follow up in the future. Some like to use a template for reflective thinking, to guide them through various steps; others are freethinkers. We have seen large leather-bound notebooks filled with flowing script, and tiny, palm-sized notebooks, elegantly written with the minimum of words.

We recommend that you re-read your journal on a regular basis. You can glance through it, or dip into it, or sit down once a month and re-read it formally. Through this process you may recognize patterns emerging, and you might find yourself formulating new ideas about old issues.

CASE STUDY

When Jane started travelling in her mid-20s, she decided to make scrapbook journals. She wanted something more visual than just using the written word. Her travel journals included written descriptions, drawings and pasted-in items such as tickets and postcards. This satisfied her visual learning style, and made it more interesting to re-read for her.

Her current reflective journals are similar to the scrapbook travel journals. She does some deep, written reflection, but includes some cut and pasted emails that she wants to reflect on, feedback forms and patients' thank-you letters. On some pages there are expressive drawings, showing circles and squares, arrows and explosions, where she wants to show a dynamic in diagram form.

In the last couple of years, she has deliberately headed each entry with a face, drawn with a felt-tipped pen and showing a smile, a down-turned mouth, a mouth open with surprise, or a confused expression. It is a quick, shorthand way of reminding herself to include cheerful entries alongside the more negative ones. It could be used as a shorthand way of recognizing the emotion of that particular event.

Jane goes to her supervisor once a month, and takes a few minutes to scan through her journal before going, in order to remind herself what has happened during the month and what she needs to talk about. She has found that, even when something is apparently resolved through self-reflection, it can often benefit from an airing in front of a supervisor. There are always new blind spots that can be opened out.

If you prefer to write on paper rather than the computer, choosing a book for your journal can be part of the reflective process. We suggest that you choose one that you will enjoy using. You can personalize it by gluing a favourite postcard or drawing on the front, or by covering it with paper or fabric of your choice. Embellish it as you like but make it a special book, that you are drawn to pick up. You might find that this experience of making the book itself will start a process of reflection.

BEGINNING THE REFLECTIVE JOURNEY

Why can't I find the book that I want?
By not finding it, am I sabotaging this project?
How does not finding what I want relate to my work?
What would happen if I just chose the one I like the most even though it is the wrong colour?
Why do I not like this colour?
How can I change the look and the colour?
I shall cover it in a red leather fabric.
Now it looks better. Now I can begin.

JOURNAL WRITING

The self-reflective journal can be used in any way that suits you, but we recommend that you balance your writing between celebrating your success and learning from your mistakes. For some people, it is easier to focus on their weaknesses rather than their strengths. The mind can run easily towards faults and failures. A journal that is written purely about negative experiences can be damaging, especially if you are just beginning to develop your inner supervisor. However, if you take time to write about what you achieved and did well, you can consolidate the good experiences and in so doing repeat your successes and enhance your self-vision. The more you write about your achievements, the more often they will happen.

Driscoll (2000), in *Practising Clinical Supervision: A Reflective Approach*, points to the value of the journal as a record-keeper.

> Writing, whether it takes the form of reflective diaries or journals, is a powerful medium for facilitating reflection on practice…and assists the supervision process by acting as a reminder and a more in-depth analysis of what went on… Apart from being a useful aide-memoire about clinical practice, recorded documentation of what goes on in the clinical supervision session is essential… Reflective writing as a preparation to the session, or as a post-session activity, allows both supervisee and supervisor to follow up any intention for practice and a useful tool for monitoring the effectiveness of clinical supervision. (p.22)

How you use the reflective journal will vary according to your current needs. You can use it regularly to review incidents from your working life. You can work from a critical incident, event or success that triggers thoughts or emotions in you. You can use it to do an audit if you feel it is time to do a review of your normal working practices. For some people, writing a journal can help them to discharge emotive events. It is a way of making sense of seemingly intractable situations and a way of lessening the personal trauma (see Box 9.1).

Box 9.1 Uses of the self-reflective journal

- Recognize what you have learned and celebrate it.

- Explore your difficulties or mistakes and identify why they happened.

- Notice your emotions and examine how they affected the situation.

- Look at any negative thoughts you may have and investigate them.

- Make an action plan about how to make changes.

- Decide what resources you might need.

Sometimes the act of self-reflection is enough to create change. But frequently there needs to be an action plan, following the self-reflection. In this you can make plans for your management of similar situations in the future. You can decide how you might change your behaviour, attitudes or values in relationships. You can set goals about how you would develop your work. This in itself will lead to another cycle of reflection.

USING A REFLECTIVE TEMPLATE

One of the simplest ways to do self-reflection is through reviewing a situation, in order to make new sense of it so that you can respond differently in the future. There are many ways in which you can involve yourself in this reviewing process. When you reflect, you can use different perspectives to come to a deeper understanding. For example, if you look at your responses to a particular situation, you might recognize your own personal attitudes and prejudices. If you take it further, you might discover an ethical aspect, or an element of comparing this situation to ones you might have met in the past. You might also look at other viewpoints on the issue, such as what the client's perspectives might be and how they might align with yours. How might this enhance or interfere with the relationship?

Some people find it easier to reflect if there is a template to follow. There are several different reflective cycles available from different authors. We would like to introduce you to our Inspire ladder template. This is loosely modelled on the children's board game of 'Snakes and Ladders', where you go up ladders and down snakes. Even though our model includes a ladder that you climb up, new situations will give you the opportunity to climb another ladder. We have represented the new situation as the arrow sending you back to the beginning again. The ladders are not aligned because the habit of reflection enables you to start reflecting from a different place each time (see Figure 9.1).

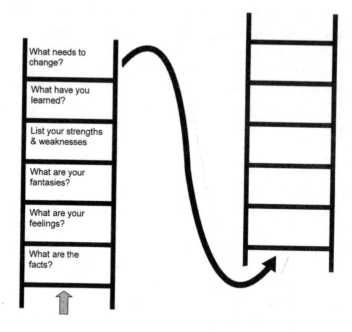

Figure 9.1 Inspire ladder template

CASE STUDY

- *What are the facts?* A woman booked in to see me with her six-year-old son, who had a continuous blocked nose and hearing difficulties that were causing problems at school. I explained what the first appointment would entail and, when she asked on the phone if she could bring her daughter as well, I requested that she make other arrangements for her. I wanted to focus on the son who was to be my patient.

  She arrived for the appointment with both son and daughter. At first both children were very well behaved, and played with the toys that I had provided. The daughter was the first to get bored, and kept coming over to me to ask me questions about my own family. I tried to redirect her to the toys, and did not answer her questions. Then the son began to get bored, and tried to investigate my room, my computer and my books. When this was refused, he began teasing his sister and some wild horseplay ensued. I found it more and more difficult to concentrate on the case.

- *What were my feelings?* I felt irritated that the mother had brought both children. I felt anxious that I would not get the information I needed. As the session progressed, I began to feel anxious for my books and computer. I felt stressed with the noisy and very physical play that was going on. I felt helpless, because it felt inappropriate to act as a schoolteacher in front of the mother. I felt indignant that I should be put in this position.

- *What were my fantasies?* I imagined that this woman had not even tried to make arrangements for her daughter. I assumed that she was trying to put me under stress so that I would sympathize with her difficult job as a mother. At the same time, I began to imagine that she was not a good mother, because she could not control her children!

- *What were my strengths and weaknesses?* I can congratulate myself that I had guessed this might possibly happen, and had produced suitable toys for both children. It has happened to me before so I could remain outwardly calm. I did the right thing in refusing to interact with the daughter, and preventing the son exploring my books and computer, because both these modelled the clear boundaries that I want to have within my consulting room.

    My weak point was that I did not explain clearly enough to the mother that the appointment would be for an hour and a half, and I needed to focus on her son. I should have explained that, in my experience, waiting for so long might be too difficult for a five-year-old girl.

- *What have I learned?* Once I took responsibility for not explaining the working agreement clearly enough, I could let go of my fantasies that the woman was deliberately causing chaos for me. I had seen her as a persecutor, and myself as a victim.

- *What needs to change?* Reflecting on this experience has taught me to make clearer contracts, and I will review over the next month how I have dealt with new patients.

Another of our models, which we call 'Other people's shoes', is a cyclical one that takes you from a description of the event and your feelings to viewing it from a different angle. The focus of this cycle is to see how other points of view may change your perspective and allow you to move forward in your thinking (see Figure 9.2).

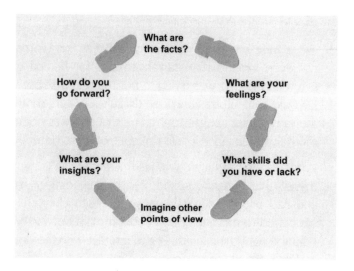

Figure 9.2 Other people's shoes template

A simple model that appeals to some people is Borton's 'Developmental model for reflective practice', which he pioneered in 1970 (Borton 1970; Jasper 2003, p.99). This is a sequential and cyclical model focusing on three questions: What? So what? Now what? The first question encourages a description of the issue including your role and that of others. The second one encourages you to reflect on your learning – for example, What did I base my actions on and what was going through my mind at the time? What could I have done differently? What is my new understanding of this situation? The final question asks you to consider how you can change your actions in the future to improve things for yourself and those around you.

You may notice that one cycle of reflection can lead on to another, and will take you to a deeper level of understanding each time. However, we suggest you give yourself permission to be flexible with any circular or linear model. Johns (2004), in *Becoming a Reflective Practitioner*, argues that fixed models may be limiting:

> My caution is that stage models immediately present reflection as some technical linear task. In a technology-driven society the risk exists that reflective models will be grasped as a technology and used in concrete ways. From a technological perspective, as opposed to a reflective perspective, the risk is that practitioners will fit their experience to the model of reflection rather than use the model creatively to guide them to see self within the context of the particular experience. (p.19)

OTHER TECHNIQUES TO TRY

There are no rules as to how to write in your journal. You could try out different techniques to explore which suit your learning style and which challenge you the most. Here are some examples.

- *Objective-subjective:* Write a factual account of a situation and then rewrite the account in a more reflective way, introducing the word 'I' and focusing on your feelings about that situation. Seeing the difference between these two ways of writing will enable you to take ownership of the situation.

- *Two columns:* Draw a vertical line down the middle of your page, or divide your screen into two columns. On one side write the narrative of what happened and on the other side write questions that have arisen from it.

- *Different points of view:* A playful way of writing is to engage with an issue from many different viewpoints. Write your own view of the situation. Then become one of the other protagonists from the original event and write what you imagine they would say about the situation. You can do this with as many of the players in the scenario as you want. Be aware that the more you feel antipathetic towards one of these people, the more useful the exercise. When you have done this, ask yourself, having heard these other points of view whether there is anything that you would have done differently; and, if so, how might you act in the future.

- *Write a poem*: You may be moved to write a poem about a particular incident that has affected you.

- *Sub-personalities*: Develop sub-personae for yourself – so for example, 'the wise man', 'the moaning minny', 'the know all', the 'I'm no good'. Write a description of an incident noticing which of your sub-personalities were present. Create helpful sub-personae to enable you to work more effectively.

- *Write to someone you know*: Some people like to personify their journal. Imagine you are writing to someone you know or to a made-up person.

- *Mind maps, lists and drawings*: If you are a visual person, you might want to include mind maps, bullet points, graphs, diagrams or drawings (see Chapter 6). Issues, dilemmas or successes can all be expressed equally well in visual forms. Drawings do not have to be naturalistic. You can use blocks of coloured shapes, lines, arrows and spirals to represent the issue, and then ask yourself questions about what you see.

Here are some questions to help you use your drawings, but feel free to develop your own.

REFLECTIVE QUESTIONS FOR DRAWINGS

- How close are the shapes to each other? What information does this tell you about the situation?

- How do the shapes relate to each other, and are some bigger and others smaller? How does this have a bearing on the interaction that you have with your client?

- Are the shapes coloured or shaded? Are they the same colour or different?

- Do you have a colour preference? Is there one that you are attracted to more than another, and is this enacted in the dynamic?

- Are the lines that you use straight or rounded? Are the marks that you have made even or dotted or faint or clear? Does this have a bearing on the issue that you are thinking about and, if so, in what way?

CASE STUDY

Jane wanted to talk about a newly formed supervision group with her supervisor. In her role as facilitator, she was finding it quite difficult to keep a balance between the three supervisees, who had very different agendas. As she reflected on this in her journal, she felt that it would be interesting to represent the dynamics as a drawing, showing how they interrelated. She used square boxes to show the seating arrangement, and spirals coming out from each box to show the energy of each member of the group (see *Figure 9.3*).

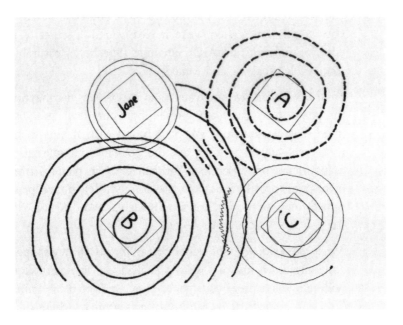

Figure 9.3 Four seats with four spirals

Jane told the supervisor that this represented the group, but did not explain in detail. She was curious to see how someone else would perceive the dynamic, so she just handed over the picture. The supervisor gave her observations, but was most interested in the spiral that came from one of the group members and overlapped Jane herself. She questioned what was going on, and Jane began to self-reflect on how the energy of one of the group members had an influence on her. As a result of this, she was no longer the neutral facilitator for the group. She could then decide on an action plan as to how to change her relationship to the group.

FURTHER USES OF THE JOURNAL

As well as being used to celebrate what you have learned, and to explore your difficulties, the journal can be used for specific tasks.

- *Goal-setting*: It is useful to do a brainstorming to identify what it is you really want, before setting goals. You can do this by using a mind map, writing or drawing all the elements. Allow yourself to dream and picture the most gorgeous outcome you would want. Then write it clearly and specifically in your journal, with SMART outcomes (Specific, Measurable, Achievable, Realistic and Timed).

- *Positive visualization*: You can make a positive visualization for yourself by creatively presenting your goal, as a list, mind map or drawing. We have found that, if you spend time creatively in writing out the goal in your journal, it helps focus your intention. You can paste in pictures from magazines to make a collage, use coloured felt-tipped pens, or use computer design accessories such as Word Art or Clip Art.

- *Newspaper headlines*: Cut out the headlines from newspapers and journals to create a positive visualization. These messages will help you achieve your goals. They work on a subliminal level and embed the possibility of achievement where once you might have had doubts. Alternatively, you can make your own messages out of different headlines put together, or by changing a word or letter.

- *Auditing:* You can use the journal to audit a particular aspect of your work, either because something is not running smoothly or as a review.

CASE STUDY

Caroline decided to explore why and when her patients phoned her. She had the impression that suddenly she was experiencing an increase in phone calls and that certain days seemed busier in terms of calls than others. She was curious to find out why. She used her journal to make a grid so she could note down which day people called and the nature of their enquiry. She made four grids and filled them in over four weeks.

She then reflected on the results. Using a reflective cycle, she asked herself what her part was in the pattern that was emerging, and how she might change her behaviour. She wondered whether the outgoing phone message on her answer-phone was inviting the number of calls that she was getting. After a month of collecting data in her journal, she analyzed the results. She decided that there probably was something about her phone message that suggested that she was always available. Her action plan was to change the wording of it and give very clear details about her availability. She then filled in grids for a second month, in order to review whether her hypothesis had been right. She discovered, to her relief, that the phone calls diminished but she still retained the same patient numbers. The result was that she felt less burdened because she was dealing with fewer calls.

THE POSITIVE ACHIEVEMENT JOURNAL

The positive achievement journal is simply a record of everything you have done well, either on a day-to-day basis or with regards to a specific topic. It is best done in a completely separate folder or book that is dedicated to self-appreciation, and not mixed up with the reflective journal, which may at times be negative.

We have found in all aspects of our work that low self-confidence may be an issue with supervisees or students. Low self-esteem can lead to a vicious cycle of low expectations and a low success rate. A positive achievement journal helps those supervisees turn the focus away from the negative, and celebrate everything they did well. Over time, this can build up confidence and raise achievement.

Positive achievements can include the smallest things, such as keeping your temper with a colleague who is irritating you, or getting to work on time. Achievements can also be tasks that you set yourself, such as regularly reading professional publications or remembering to do your computer back-up.

Peer groups

While the journal is invaluable for use between supervision sessions or if the supervisor is not available, the other alternative is the peer group. Peer groups are set up between like-minded people as support groups, supervision groups, or cross-professional groups. Sometimes they are set up out of financial necessity, or from a desire for independence.

Peer groups can, at their best, be supportive places to reflect, and give and receive supervision. They can be a fertile place to learn and share together. The group can organize itself as it wants and can create flexibility around time, frequency of meetings, or venue. They are generally non-hierarchical and each member can take it in turns to lead or chair so that nobody holds long-term responsibility for the group.

Peer groups are a potentially creative space where you can practice all the techniques mentioned in this book as well as making up some of your own. This includes using your journal. However, peer groups need careful organization. If the group members have limited experience of supervision, they might have an unclear working agreement or loose boundaries; there might be group collusion or one member might challenge the group. We recommend that the whole group creates a clear working agreement on the first day of meeting, and has regular reviews (see Box 9.2).

CONSIDER EVERYONE'S DEVELOPMENTAL STAGE

Some groups work really well, with all the participants at different developmental stages. Even if some of them are new to their profession and others are mature in their profession, they can still find things to learn from each other. This is because everyone has different life

---

Box 9.2 Setting up a peer group

• Consider everyone's developmental stage.

• Clarify the vision of the group.

• Set up a group working agreement, to include regular meeting times.

• Agree an agenda at the beginning of each meeting.

• Review the group's needs regularly.

---

experiences or different abilities or willingness to reflect. Other groups might want equality, with a similarity between the skills, experience and learning of each. If some participants are more mature in experience or skills than others, they may end up teaching or leading the group. This is satisfying in itself, if they want to do it, but they themselves may not receive any meaningful supervision.

CLARIFY THE VISION OF THE GROUP AND MAKE A WORKING AGREEMENT

In the first session of the group, we recommend that everyone clarifies their own wants, needs and fears, so that the group can develop both an aim and a working agreement. The aim doesn't need to be complicated. It can be as simple as 'to supervise each other on our work as practitioners' or 'to reflect on how we can best promote our business'.

The working agreement needs to include practical issues such as dates, time, venue and money, if relevant. It also needs to include group values such as respect and confidentiality, as well as attending to listening and feedback skills. Decisions need to be made about the possibilities of a rotating chair, who will act as timekeeper or initiate the work.

AGREE AN AGENDA AT THE BEGINNING OF EACH MEETING

We suggest that you set aside time for arrivals and welcoming chat. There are different models of how to begin a group meeting. You can wait for someone to speak spontaneously, but we don't recommend this method because it favours the most confident people in the group. Other ways of starting are the 'temperature reading' (see Chapter 10, p.163) or all the participants can do a brief check-in of what they would like to work with. This should be done in the form of a headline without going into the content of the issue. From this, the group can decide how the timing is going to be organized.

Another useful technique for starting is to allow all the group members in turn to 'dump' any issues or baggage that they are carrying when they come to the session. This is different and distinct from work issues – it is related to what is bothering them now. For example, when Caroline was in a group and asked if she wanted to let go of something, she said, 'I am furious that I am late as my car would not start and now I am going to have to waste my time getting it sorted.' Just having the space to say that allowed her to be present in the group, let go of this issue and focus on her professional work. This material could be imagined as something that is placed in the middle of the room and then let out of the window, transformed into a puff of smoke. This technique stops chat, brings people up to date with each other's preoccupations and allows a space where the issue is left and not examined. It is simply information.

REVIEW THE GROUP'S NEEDS REGULARLY

Group awareness is important for the healthy working of a group. For example, if an issue has run over time, the group can question whether this was useful for the members and, if so, why. They may look at redressing the balance on another occasion. Sometimes one member's needs are more pressing than another's, and the group's sensitivity and ability to be flexible and responsive to this are helpful. Naming that this is what is going on can allow other members to take their turn on other occasions. As trust builds up, flexibility will increase.

Reviews should be done regularly, in order to give everyone the opportunity to express how they feel the group is progressing. This is a leaderless group, so it is worthwhile noticing the group dynamics. Are all the group members equally respectful to each other? Does everyone have a fair amount of time for their needs? Is one member taking over the group? Here are some different methods of doing a review.

- *Let the puppets speak*: If you have a collection of puppets or soft toys, these can be used to express the views of each member of the group. It can be liberating to talk through a puppet, who is often able to be more outspoken than the puppet master. Alternatively, you can work with two puppets for each group member. One puppet is the good guy who says something positive, and the other puppet is the bad guy who says something controversial.

- *Sit in a circle*: All the participants sit in a circle, preferably on chairs of equal height, and take it in turn to present their own review of how the previous few months have felt for them. Ensure everyone has the same timeslot.

- *Temperature reading*: This provides a formal structure for expressing the balance between positive and negative feelings (see Chapter 10, p.163).

- *Group mind map*: This works best on a really large piece of paper, such as flipchart paper. The group itself should be represented in the centre of the page, and everyone takes turns in adding positive and negative points in the form of a mind map. If everyone can be completely honest and congruent, some of these pointers might be conflicting, but the mind map will indeed represent the feelings of the group.

CASE STUDY

Caroline was in a peer group where four of them, including Caroline, had agreed to team teach the rest of the group. The four of them decided that they would negotiate by email as to how they would present the material to the rest of the group. Caroline sent the first email to the others in the team but only one responded. Together they formulated a plan for the group, dividing the teaching into four tasks. Caroline suggested that each of them rang one of the other two to see how they felt about the plan. There were huge apologies for being out of touch from one member who was keen to adopt the plan. She also made a suggestion of meeting a little earlier than the rest of the group so as to firm up on the roles each of them were to play in the presentation. The fourth member had sent a short email to say 'keep me in the loop'. Three of the team had chosen their roles and the fourth had not responded.

By taking a proactive role, Caroline had taken on the role of a leader even though the roles had not been discussed. She also ended up leading her three colleagues in teaching the peer group.

We can see from this case study that, if roles are not clearly delineated at the beginning, the leadership role will default to the person who has the most time, energy or experience. That person may also be the most conscientious, regardless of adequate spare time.

If you get someone who does not engage – for example, the participant who said 'keep me in the loop' – then the others may feel a number of things. The group may feel that the absentee is not pulling her weight, they may imagine she is unwell, they may resent having to spend time trying to get a response from her as well as being left to do all the planning or work. It is useful not to jump to conclusions in situations like this but to wait until there is a face-to-face discussion.

DIFFERENT METHODS OF WORKING WITHIN A GROUP

We suggest that any of the creative methods in this book would add an exciting and challenging element to a peer support group. Pen and paper can be used spontaneously. Methods that depend on props might need a little more forethought. If you keep a reflective journal, it can be useful to bring it along to the group. You can write notes in it as the work progresses, or you can use it as a reminder of what you want to work on. You could read out one of your entries and get a peer to supervise you on the issues that emerge.

Sometimes it is difficult to keep to the working agreement, and one or two group members might not keep to the task. For example, they prefer to exchange news rather than work, they overrun their timeslot, or their feedback to another member is not fair and balanced. If this happens you can ask for time-out. This is usually accompanied by the gesture of placing the hands in the shape of a 'T'. Time-out means that the current work is frozen in time, while another issue is discussed. During the time-out, the group can reconnect with the working agreement.

Give yourself permission

Developing your inner supervisor through self-reflection, writing a journal and working with your peers will enable you to learn about yourself and you will find your work more satisfying. Give yourself permission to step outside your busy week and reflect on what has happened, both good and bad. Looking at why something has gone well can consolidate good work, or give clues as to how you might work in the future in different conditions. Looking at a negative issue or a dilemma helps you plan for the future and decide what needs to be enhanced and developed. We suggest you have a regular date with your journal, your computer or your peers to keep you in touch with the processes of self-reflection and self-supervision. Play as much as you like and, if you find a critical voice creeping in, develop an alter ego that is more nurturing and tempers that voice.

Chapter 10

Beginnings, Endings, Ritual and Ceremony

When the white rabbit in Carroll's (1865) *Alice's Adventures in Wonderland* reads out the prisoner's evidence, he asks the king, 'Where shall I begin, please your Majesty?' and the king replies, 'Begin at the beginning and go on till you come to the end: then stop.' Even here in the topsy-turvy world of Alice with its strange courtroom procedures, one thing is clear: knowing that there is a beginning and an ending is important. There are moments as a supervisor that can feel as unsettling as the landscape of Alice's adventures, but creating clearly defined beginnings and endings can help you and your supervisee feel grounded.

Here we look at the opening and closing stages that take place when working in supervision. Other chapters in the book deal with the content of the supervision session itself, while this chapter focuses on the beginnings and endings that encircle those sessions or series of sessions.

In many situations, it is all too easy to slip into relationships without having a conscious insight into when or how they began or ended. This can happen in many different settings, such as with colleagues within the same organization, fellow students, neighbours, acquaintances and even friends. But when the relationship has a designated professional purpose, as it does within the supervisory context, then clearly delineating and planning beginnings and endings can create safety, reassurance and respect for both parties.

There is a clear parallel between the beginning and ending of a supervision session; and the supervisees' own experience of beginning and ending their work with their own clients or students. We have written this chapter from the point of view of the supervisor because your own clear demarcation of beginnings and endings will serve as a model for your supervisees to use in their own work with their clients and students.

We look at the opening or beginning of the session or the relationship in its fullest sense. We consider what the supervisor can do before even meeting their supervisee, how to set up the relationship, and how to use ritual to consolidate the relationship or separate from it. We address this both on a one-to-one basis as well as with a group. Finally, we look at ending a single session, and the closure of a series of sessions.

Preparing for supervision

As the supervisor you need to prepare yourself before anyone arrives, and ideally this will happen on several different levels. On an organizational level, you might find it helpful to read up on your notes or recap on the previous session. On a practical level, you might need to assemble or prepare some of your props.

You might want to clear your mind of all the work done previously in the day, in order to be present, open and focused for whatever arises in the forthcoming session. Supervision could be compared to playing a ball game, where mental acuity and emotional calm are necessary but you still don't know which way the ball will be coming from.

Sometimes sitting quietly for a few minutes and focusing on the breath with your feet firmly planted on the ground can help empty the mind. You can make a simple ritual of clearing your desk, and opening the window or door. Putting away the notes from the previous session physically removes other supervisees and clients from the working arena, and emotionally it enables you to enter the next session without carrying thoughts of the previous one.

The following rituals can be used by the supervisor prior to the session, or they can be done together with the group or supervisee.

ENHANCING RITUALS

Enhancing rituals aim to focus your energy and attention in the present moment. They heighten physical, emotional and sensory awareness.

- *Lighting a candle*: Some people like to light a candle, which acts to set the scene. Candles have many symbolic meanings, such as enlightenment and peace, as well as being used in many religions. They can act as a spiritual reminder. Other meanings are about illumination, transparency and lighting up the darkness, all of which can apply to supervision. You can discuss with the supervisee or group whether to keep the candle lit throughout the session.

- *Changing the room*: You can change the atmosphere of the room by moving furniture, opening the window or introducing meditation objects such as a bowl of shells or stones.

- *Your special senses*: Imagine yourself standing in an open space in nature. Allow your senses to come into play – for example, you could notice the wind in your hair, the sun on your face, the smell of flowers or freshly cut grass, the sound of birdsong or the taste of the picnic you have in front of you. A visualization like this will open up your awareness of what is outside you. If you don't like using visualization, then sit quietly for a moment and touch your lips, nose, eyelids, ears and your opposite hand to remind yourself of your senses, and thereby your wider awareness.

PROTECTIVE RITUALS

Sometimes working with a client or supervisee can leave one or both people feeling drained and exhausted. This can happen if you are working with difficult or stressful material. It can also occur if one of you is highly sensitive to the atmosphere or energy of the other. If you are aware that this is a possibility, a protection ritual might be useful before working with the person, to create a boundary.

CASE STUDY

In teaching practitioner development to students, Jane came across a student who was considering leaving university without completing her degree, because she found whenever she was in front of a patient she developed an intense headache. She found it was less painful if she could have a computer open in front of her, with the screen creating a barrier between them.

Jane arranged for a tutorial with the student, and it became clear that the student was highly sensitive to the atmosphere of the patients. Jane advised her to work a lot with ritual, protecting herself before the patient arrived, and using closing rituals afterwards.

Figure 10.1 Three people who draw circles in the air

Here are some examples of protective rituals.

- *Three circles in the air:* Standing upright, draw three circles in the air around you. One passes around you from side to side, one from front to back, and one around your waist (see Figure 10.1).

- *The safety of a sleeping bag:* Another version is to visualize yourself inside a large and comfortable sleeping bag. Slowly zip yourself in, starting with the feet, and taking it right over the head. (You can visualize air holes if you are claustrophobic.) If you don't like doing visualization, draw the sleeping bag in the air, around you.

• *A peaceful bubble* Take a few minutes to sit quietly, listening as you breath deeply into the abdomen. Then visualize yourself inside a safe, peaceful bubble of the colour of your choice. You can visualize the other person in another bubble of a different colour.

Beginning the relationship

In our experience, the setting up of a formal relationship with a contract or working agreement creates the best working environment for teaching or supervision. Both parties can express their own wants and needs, and it is the role of the facilitator to set the boundaries of time, space, fees, etc. (see Chapter 1). Setting up an effective working agreement in a group is slightly more complex and time consuming because there are more people to give input.

CASE STUDY

Jane was teaching a group of university students about the practitioner-patient relationship. She wanted them to think carefully about the patient's autonomy and ability to consent to treatment. She asked the students to reflect on any relationship that they had had with a practitioner in which they had felt disempowered. The practitioner could be a doctor, dentist, counsellor, consultant or a complementary therapist.

Then she asked the students to collect two or three animals from the toy box to represent that practitioner and themselves as a patient. Then they had to work in pairs, showing their choice of animals and telling as much or as little of the story as they wanted. Jane wanted the students to reflect and remember, in order for them to fully appreciate the necessity of contracting with their patients. However, she was aware that some of the stories might touch on highly sensitive issues, and remembering these might open up deep pools of emotion. Using animals to enact the situation, or even to stand in a tableau, brought distance and humour to the subject as well as insight.

The animals chosen showed a lack of equality in size and aggression. In many cases, the practitioner was shown as some overwhelming animal, like a dinosaur, a giraffe or a large bear. This made the students feel as if they were victims. If there had been a clearer contract at the beginning of the relationship, the two animals might have been represented as similar in size.

BEGINNING A ONE-TO-ONE SESSION

If you are working with individual supervisees, each session can be started in a variety of different ways. The supervisees can be invited to get straight down to work by headlining the topics that they will want to present. Alternatively, the first five or ten minutes can be spent creatively, getting the supervisees to reflect on what mood they are in, or how their week or month has gone. Here are a few suggestions.

- *Full and empty:* Ask the supervisees what they are full of, and what they are empty of. For example, 'I am full of enthusiasm for my new project, but I am empty of new clients.'

- *Find the metaphor:* Ask the supervisees for a metaphor to describe their feelings during the previous week. For example, 'I felt like a snail, moving slowly, and every so often I would retreat into my home.'

- *Making a drawing:* Get the supervisees to do a quick drawing, using coloured shapes to represent the different issues that they have brought. Get them to emphasize the size, shape and colour of the issues, so that it becomes clear which is the key one that they want to focus on first.

BEGINNING A SESSION WITH A GROUP

For many people small, opening rituals can create familiarity and security. They enable the supervisee or group to let go of the outside world, and focus inwards on the supervision work. This is particularly so with groups, which have the dual task of doing some effective supervision for themselves and enabling the supervision of others. Opening rituals can take about ten or fifteen minutes.

For some groups it is appropriate to do a warm-up exercise as an opener. In a workshop situation, an example would be introducing your neighbour to the group or throwing a ball around the group calling out your own name and the name of the person to whom you are throwing it. All these exercises will help everyone to remember each other's name and are good for group bonding. Other groups need a calming ritual, to help everyone focus inwardly, making them more self-reflective. For example, a gentle opening ritual can be a relaxation exercise, which can optionally be followed by a visualization.

For a gentle opening ritual, begin by asking the group to sit quietly, cross-legged or with their feet on the ground. They may want to take their shoes off. Suggest that they might like to close their eyes, or relax them by looking at something calming. Get them to focus on their breathing and, once this has been established for a few minutes, you might choose to introduce other ideas. Suggest they give themselves permission to let go of the journey they have just been on. You can ask them to allow an image to appear or you might ask them what they need from this session. Thus it can be used either as a pure relaxation to prepare for work or, as in the case of the image work, it can act as a springboard for the entire session.

Another kind of opener that can be used at the beginning of sessions is that of a 'temperature reading'. This is a model that was devised by the family therapist Virginia Satir (1988, p.289). Originally used in family therapy, it is now widely used in organizational group work and can be adapted for use in any group supervision session. According to the nature of the group, the facilitator needs to decide how long each member will speak.

There are five elements to it: appreciation, new information, puzzles, complaints with recommendations, and wishes, hopes and dreams. Each person in the group takes it in turns to go through these five elements in relation to their work. Appreciations can be in relation to the group itself, so, for example, someone who brought cherries to a session, or humour, might receive appreciation from a group member in the following session. New information may be a place for sharing both new professional and personal information. Puzzles could be about anything, such as a group situation or a client, or could form the basis of the issue that someone is bringing. Complaints with recommendations could be about the group or work.

Wishes, hopes and dreams helps the group members focus towards their goals. Encourage everyone to speak from the first person, to create ownership of what they are saying.

The 'temperature reading' can act as a quick way of knowing where all group members are at the moment, what has happened to them in the intervening period, what material they bring and what they hope to achieve.

Making an ending

There are many different sorts of endings. There is the ending of the session, and the ending of a series of sessions, which is often called closure. We look at these separately, but the strategies and rituals that we recommend can be interchanged. Finally, we look at what happens to the supervisor after the end of the session.

Time management of the session is the responsibility of the supervisor or facilitator. Occasional time checks are useful for everyone, and the approaching ending should be flagged up. There should be the opportunity to have a few minutes for reviewing the work done, either verbally or in a reflective journal. Here are some suggestions for strategies or rituals for ending a session.

- *Reflecting on strengths and weaknesses*: Ask everyone to reflect on their strengths and weaknesses from the session, either in the reflective journal or by saying it out loud to the rest of the group.

- *Consider the themes*: Ask everyone to think about the session and consider what themes have emerged for them. This can reveal ideas about what to take forward to the next meeting.

- *Find a word*: If you had started with a 'temperature reading', you can ask for one word from each of the group to encapsulate how each person feels at the end of the session.

CLOSURE: THE ENDING OF A RELATIONSHIP

The end of a relationship, where two people have worked together as practitioner-client, teacher-student or supervisor-supervisee, benefits from a closing ceremony. Creating an official ending allows closure, mentally, emotionally and physically. A good ending will allow both participants to take something away with them in the form of a verbal appreciation or something written. It creates a sense of ceremony, which can help the supervisee acknowledge their achievement.

There might be some practical demands before the closure of a relationship. For example, the supervisor might have to write a report, or the student might have to present a portfolio. Beyond this, it is useful and transparent if both people can have the opportunity to review what they have gained from the relationship. What has been learned needs to be acknowledged. You can refer back to the original working agreement, and check whether all the desired outcomes have been achieved. If anything feels missing or incomplete, now will be the time to voice this. Here are some methods of closure with individual supervisees or students.

- *Completing the work*: When working one-to-one, a short closing ceremony is to ask the supervisees to sit quietly and breathe deeply for a few minutes, and then ask them if there is anything they would like to say or do, to make them feel complete before leaving.

- *Make a list*: Say or write a list of things you appreciate about each other. In this instance, closure can be an opportunity for celebration and congratulation.

Group closure

When a group is ending, the participants may feel a whole range of emotions that might include grief, excitement about the future or emotional numbness. Allow people space to express their feelings. Proctor (2000), in *Group Supervision: A Guide to Creative Practice*, emphasizes the importance of this moment in a group's life:

If the group has done good work together it will have become a significant life experience for the supervisees. Disruptions and endings can cause grief and anxiety which seem out of proportion for a 'task group'. The supervisor, who may already be gearing up for the next 'intake', should take time to appreciate the ending (or change) of this human system. Coming changes or group demise should be signalled well ahead and suitable leave-taking rituals co-operatively planned. (p.106)

As a group disbands, there can be a feeling of vulnerability, similar to the feelings when a group is forming. The group has been witness to the changes and self-development of each individual and, with the loss of the group, there can be a sense of a loss of identity. The group members need the time to honour the work they have done together, and their joint and individual journeys of self-discovery. It is also helpful for them to look forward to their future and what they take with them from the group experience. Here are some ideas for closing ceremonies that help acknowledge the work done and soften the separation that is about to occur.

- *Appreciation*: Go round the group and get everyone to appreciate something about the group and the time that they have spent in it.

- *Leaving present*: Ask everyone in the group to provide a goodbye gift for the others. This can be a suggestion, an appreciation, an evaluation, a visualization, a sharing of information or anything else.

- *Then and now*: Have a selection of toy animals (see Chapter 4). Tip them into the centre of the group and ask all participants to choose two animals. One animal will represent how they saw themselves at the formation of the group and the other represents them now. They will take it in turns to share their development via the animals. This can create insights and humour, both of which are helpful when a group is ending.

- *Paper chains*: An uplifting, colourful ceremony is to provide coloured paper, scissors and glue or staplers. Get the group members to cut out strips and make paper chains. They need to make a chain big enough that they can hold it within a circle. Once it is made, get the group in a circle; each person should be holding a piece of the chain. You can go round the circle appreciating each other and then pull the chain apart, leaving each person with a part of the chain to take away.

- *Values cards*: Another ceremony is to place a pile of blank-coloured business cards in the centre of a circle with some coloured pens. All participants take a card and a pen and write on the card a value that they would like to give to someone in the group. For example, people might write down courage, determination, insight, ambition or any other qualities that they may wish to give to others. Either they can give them out directly or a more dynamic version is to put them in a box and pass them round for everyone to take a lucky dip.

For most situations, the process of closure includes a review of what has been learned and appreciation of what went well. A brief ceremony gives a sense of completion and moving on. Something light-hearted, such as an opportunity to play together, can be appropriate for diffusing the seriousness or intensity of the work done previously. In some cases, where a relationship has not been satisfactory, for closure to be useful it needs to include an acknowledgement of this. In the following case example, the closure focused on recognizing and re-balancing the heightened emotions felt by a group of students.

CASE STUDY

Jane was asked to teach in a small college, but unfortunately after a year it went bankrupt and had to close down. The students were extremely upset and angry, because they felt they had been abandoned before completing their course.

At the end of term, Jane arranged for a group closure ceremony. She wanted everyone to be able to move forward, on their chosen path of home study or joining another college, without carrying the resentment of this experience.

She asked everyone to sit comfortably, and take some time to be quiet and grounded. She asked them to cast their mind over the time they had spent in the college, and remember two events. One was to be something that they would treasure and remember with gratitude. The other was to be something that they really disliked about the college, even before the bankruptcy and abrupt closure. Everyone was given plenty of time to choose two issues, and then Jane asked them to come back to the present.

She gave them paper and coloured felt-tipped pens and explained what she wanted them to do. The positive memory was to be written on a large piece of paper with a glowing description, enhanced with decorations, and taken home. The negative memory was to be written on a smaller piece of paper, and twisted into a tight ball. Jane set up a tray, with a circle of tea lights and, with due caution to fire regulations, she lit them and asked everyone to place their negative ball into the centre of the fiery circle. If they had been outside, Jane might have asked everyone to actually burn their negative memories, but this ritual was a safer option for inside.

Afterwards, Jane asked everyone to stand up and brush their body down with their hands, as the final cleansing from such a negative experience. The atmosphere on finishing was noticeably lighter, with some students peacefully quiet and others sharing jokes and reminding each other of happier times.

A ceremony like this cannot change the facts of the situation. The students were still being abruptly evicted from their college. But it is hoped that the ritual allowed them to let go of any resentment that they may have harboured in relation to studying, and would allow them to enjoy learning in the future.

After the supervision session

After the supervisee or group have left, you might need to do a mental review, make some notes in your records or do some self-reflection in your journal. You might also want to do a simple closing ritual, especially if you began the session with an enhancing ritual to open up your awareness.

Closing rituals are not always necessary, and will depend as much on the sensitivity of the supervisor as the content of the session.

- *Freshening up*: A simple closing ritual is to open the windows and doors to let a flow of air through the room, wash your hands, or put away the notes.

- *Space clearing*: The next two suggestions come from space-clearing techniques, using sound to change the vibrations in the room. You can ring a bell or bang a gong, standing in the centre of the room. Or you can clap your hands, going around the room clapping high and low and as close to the wall as possible.

- *The body brush*: Stand away from any furniture and start brushing down your body with your hands, starting with the head and making brisk sweeping movements over the torso and limbs.

Safety and security

Appropriate beginnings and endings create safety, reassurance and respect for the supervisee. If you plan how to open and close each session, as well as the series of sessions, you'll find that the supervision runs more smoothly. It also creates a good working model for the supervisee to copy, whether consciously or unconsciously. All the methods and suggestions given in this chapter can be used either for yourself, or for a group or individual supervisee.

Chapter 11

Working at a Distance

Can you remember as a child being asked to write a letter to a penpal, or a distant relative whom you could not remember ever having met? You probably found it difficult to write if you did not have a strong sense of the other person, A similar sense of isolation can be felt by those working on distance-learning programmes. This feeling lessens as you start to communicate with someone. It is the same when you are working at a distance with a supervisee whom you have not met.

This chapter looks at how, by using technological advances, you can work effectively at a distance. This works for people who are geographically distant from an appropriate supervisor, using the phone, email and internet video connections. However, these are reliant on both the machinery and the service providers working well. The advantages are global accessibility, flexibility of working and sometimes cultural diversity.

Distance supervision works best when skills and knowledge are already embedded from previous supervision experiences, even if both people have never met before. For example, it can work well if both people have had supervision experience, or the supervisor is confident in the methodology, or the supervisee is familiar with the skills of self-reflection. These form solid foundations that balance the sensory deprivation of distance work. However, we always recommend face-to-face sessions for people coming into supervision for the first time, to give them support while they are learning self-reflective skills.

For the supervisor there are the pleasures of working with a wider range of people and even getting to know new cultures. As with all the techniques in this book, we recommend careful contracting, before you start. The disadvantages for the supervisor are that they miss out on a lot of the non-verbal and intuitive observations that they would get from sitting in front of the supervisee.

Telephone supervision

Phone conversations are completely verbal, with a loss of visual clues, although they still have aural non-verbal communication, such as the tone of voice and the choice of words used. Generally, because of the lack of visual connection, most people feel free to talk on the phone while walking, travelling or doing any other task at the same time. If the phone call is for supervision purposes, there needs to be a total commitment to the session. Both of you need to sit somewhere where you are not overheard, distracted or interrupted and can talk reflectively and openly. We do not recommend text messaging for supervision, because this method naturally contracts thought into the shortest possible words. Supervision needs to have a modality in which it can develop and expand both thought and words.

There will be a natural inclination to use verbal supervision styles on the phone, such as discussion, and a tendency to move away from visual creative supervision. We suggest you use a range of different intervention styles to maximize dialogue, ensuring that it extends beyond discussion into a meaningful supervisory process. Consider using a methodology such as 'conversations inviting change' (see Chapter 7, p.110). Creative exercises can be set for the supervisee to do alone, with a follow-up phone call arranged to discuss them.

The advantage of phone supervision is that it is immediate and the discussion can flow easily and spontaneously. It works best if both people have already met face-to-face in a supervisory context.

Email supervision

Email uses written communication but can include some visual elements if a drawing, diagram or photo is attached. There is a lack of face-to-face communication, so again visual, non-verbal clues are missing. There cannot be absolute security with email so, if clients are being discussed, extra care should be taken that they are not named or identifiable.

Email supervision does not take place in real time and there can be considerable time lapses between the supervisor's intervention and the reply, especially when both people live in different continents. This can result in a lack of spontaneity, but on the other hand the slow pace may be appreciated by those who are working in a different language and need time to find the right words. We suggest that you make an agreement between both of you about how promptly you will write back, so that neither loses the thread of the discussion. The supervisor can keep records of how much time they are spending on each session so that fees can be calculated accordingly.

The advantages of email supervision are that the natural time lapses can be extended to use any of the creative supervision techniques. You can set small tasks, explaining what you want the supervisee to do, and using links to other internet functions as a way of clarifying your meaning. For example, when working across language and cultural differences, misunderstandings due to mistranslations are possible. It is quick and effective to include a link to a picture that shows what you intend. If supervisees have used toys, objets trouvés or any other three-dimensional props, they can take digital photos and send them to you.

By the end of the supervision session, the entire discussion is on record, available for cutting and pasting into the reflective journal for future re-reading. Photos can be kept as a reminder, or even put up as the computer wallpaper, to act as a positive visualization.

Internet video supervision

Video supervision can be dependent on the quality of the connection, which at the time of writing can vary from day to day. The video session takes place in real time, so both people can access the verbal and visual clues that are in view of the camera, such as facial expression, eye contact and body language. However, it is dependent upon both the equipment and the service provider working well. If the work is being done across continents, email has to be used beforehand to set an appropriate start time that works across both time zones.

All the creative supervision styles can be used. For example, the supervisees can be encouraged to use toys and objets trouvés to create a constellation, and the whole of this process will be live on video. They can make a drawing, create a poem or design a chart, and during times of silence the supervisor can still make observations.

We suggest that a conscious effort should be made to make notes, either during or after the session. For some people note taking is automatic in a face-to-face session, but the intensity of a video session may cause them to forget.

Setting supervision tasks

You can use creative supervision with all three of these distance methods. Often it is more effective to set tasks or exercises for supervisees to do in their own time, and to follow these up with a phone, internet or email session. The supervisees will need to provide their own props, so your instructions about these need to be flexible, allowing them to work with what is available. Some of your tasks might be new to the supervisees, so you should give your instructions very clearly and concisely. This can be done as an email attachment so that it is available should they need to refer to it again in the future. For example:

> First I would like you to collect up a pile of small objects. For example, these could be toys, small Christmas decorations, souvenirs or natural objects like shells or small stones. It would be good if you could find about 20 objects or more.
>
> Next, please sit down quietly with all the objects in front of you on a table or on the floor and bring your issue to mind. Choose one or several objects that will represent yourself, and some objects for any other people who are part of this issue. You can include anything else, if you feel it will help.
>
> Finally, place the objects very carefully in relationship to each other. How far apart should they be? How close? Allow yourself to be intuitive about this and work with what feels right. Don't think too much.

Please send me a photo of this arrangement or a written description, and then we will explore what you can learn from it.

Some supervisees prefer to do one task at a time, reflecting on it carefully before moving on, while others are stimulated by being given complex or multiple tasks. In the following case example, several different small tasks were given as a way of exploring new ways of working.

CASE STUDY

A homeopathic practitioner living in New Zealand emailed Jane asking for some help with her case analysis style. She wrote:

> I would like to think about my analysis pattern. It's very cluttered and confusing, and after the end of every case analysis, I have to sweep up the debris. I am totally exhausted, and my brain is aching. I am sure that after more experience, I will be able to do better, but at the same time I have begun to feel that I'm doing it in a way that I'm not good at. I have been thinking about my working style, which I originally thought was doing research and analysis, but I have started to doubt it. I would like something more dynamic. Can you suggest some other ways of working?

Jane decided to use two different interventions (see Heron's (1990) interventions, Chapter 1, p. 19). She would be informative and make suggestions about how the supervisee could use more structure in her work. She would balance this with a catalytic intervention using five different creative supervision tasks. These would encourage the supervisee to explore different ways of working. Jane wrote:

> I suggest that you take an old case, and try out all of these different systems, and then do some self-reflection about which ones are good for you. Keep an open mind, and if my suggestions produce more ideas for you to work in even more different ways, then try them out.

The supervisee wrote back after 24 hours. She did not give any details of the case, which was not necessary. However, it is interesting to see how the client's personality had a clear impact on each supervision technique.

- *Acting out the client*: I came into the room with a kind of fearful or suspicious look, 'What are you going to do with me?' I was restless with limited eye contact.

- *Drawing*: I painted a watercolour veil and lots of red spots behind the veil. The red spots are sparks that say 'CAUTION-BURN'. The red spots are extending into my space, the boundaries are too low. I am a yellow box which is smouldering from the heat. I need to create stronger boundaries!

- *Talking to the client from the practitioner's chair*: I hope you express yourself honestly. You must be feeling that you are a victim of your controlling boss, and your female colleagues. I can see you hold lots of anger inside you. It's very interesting that you weep so much in front of me, but it seems you only want to tell me what you want, and you order me what to do.

- *Talking to the practitioner from the client's chair*: Why do I have to put up with so much, it's always me who carries the burden! No one understands me, not even my family! I was left out of my family, because my mother and my sister were so close, and I couldn't get in. Nobody listens to me! Nobody listens properly! I don't want to talk about it, just listen to what I tell you!

- *Visualization on a desert island:* I was in my house near a beautiful lake and doing meditation, preparing to create a good atmosphere. I was happy with the energy in me and the surroundings. Suddenly there was a knock at the door and my client was there. She saw me and said to me, 'I don't like this atmosphere, I hate women who look happy.'

The supervisee then reflected on how she felt using all these techniques. Some of them confirmed what she had already known, and some helped her to understand the client better. Her greatest enjoyment was doing the drawing and her greatest learning was the visualization, which she found quite shocking because it was so unexpected. Her final comment was: 'All through the creative work, I felt this was a great tool to detach myself from the energy of the client. It was a sort of cleansing.'

Jane wrote back to express her pleasure in reading through the results of her suggestions. The supervisee had worked through the different creative techniques, wholeheartedly, and used self-reflection to identify what would be the most effective for her in the future.

The role of the supervisor

In previous chapters, we have written about different aspects of the supervisor's role, such as negotiating the working agreement or offering both support and challenge. Some of these skills are easily transferable to distance supervision. A clear working agreement or contract needs to be formed. Different intervention styles can be used to offer support and challenge.

The main difference in the supervisor's role in distance work will be in how they create and maintain an effective relationship with the supervisee. When two people are in the same room, this is frequently done through non-verbal signals and social conventions. For example, these include the smile on arrival, the handshake, the nod in agreement or the open body language. Many of these are lost with distance supervision and without them supervisees might feel vulnerable, detached from the process or unwilling to reflect deeply, because they don't feel held in the same way. We suggest you need to make an extra effort to keep the supervisees feeling supported. This might mean giving more positive feedback than you would normally, focusing in particular on your appreciation of their ability to work with different methodologies. In other words, it is the engagement rather than the results that need encouragement.

The experience of the supervisor, doing distance supervision, is that the piece of work does not progress smoothly. It starts and then stops, especially with email. You can give your input enthusiastically but then you have to wait to find out whether your suggestions have been understood, and whether they have been acted on. There can at times be misunderstandings, particularly when there are cultural and language differences, and you have to be patient and work with whatever presents itself. Occasionally the supervisee can put a lot of effort into doing a piece of work that, because of a misunderstanding, was not what you asked for. With distance supervision you have to go with the flow, probably more than in face-to-face situations. You need to accept that there will be as much or more learning from the 'mistake' as there would have been had the supervisee followed your instructions as you had intended. As a result of this added complexity, you will probably have a lot to reflect on in your journal.

If you suggest any of the creative supervision techniques and the supervisee agrees to do these and get back to you later, you have to give your instructions and then let go. When you're working face-to-face, you are on hand to provide the props and the encouragement. In the last case study, Jane wanted to suggest the visualization, but was very uncertain how this would work with the supervisee reading it to herself and then visualizing it. Her experience had always been that the supervisor or facilitator spoke the visualization to a more passive, listening supervisee. With phone supervision, you could read supervisees the visualization and let them respond as you would with a supervisee in the room. In the event, handing over the visualization to the supervisee was very effective.

CASE STUDY

A newly registered practitioner moved from Canada to another country and wanted to set up a new practice there. We will call the supervisee Clara. Clara had four strategies that she implemented within the first six months of moving. These were to set up a new website, to make fliers and business cards, to run an information workshop about her work and to attend a few workshops on related topics so that she could make contacts. However, she felt setting up a practice was an uphill task because she did not have a network base and was starting from scratch. She was not getting the new clients or referrals that she would have liked. She emailed Jane, asking for supervision.

Jane began by asking questions about the four strategies, so that she could fully understand what had been done. She asked in particular about Clara's strengths and weaknesses, encouraging her to self-reflect on her achievements to date. When she had done this, Jane was able to move into a more active and challenging role. She asked Clara to do three tasks, and write back. These were:

- to reflect further about how she advertised her information workshop, and whether she was collecting up a mailing list of interested people

- to create a pie chart, showing how she divided up her week between her part-time job, housework, time with friends, her emerging practice and so on

- to make a list of all that she had to offer a new client in terms of knowledge, skills, abilities and client relationship.

The answers came back after a few days, and Jane was very pleased to see that Clara had committed herself to honest reflection, and was already moving forward. The challenge to reflect about her workshop made Clara realize that she needed to create a mailing list and advertise more widely. She made a pie chart and the results startled her. She said, 'I had thought I spent more time on my new practice, but in truth the time is taken up elsewhere.' Finally, in making the list of reasons why a new client would choose her, she could only find two reasons, and her email sounded quite depressed. She made a list of all the qualities she was lacking, and dwelt on two clients whose cases seemed incomplete. It was clear that further work needed to be done in this area.

Jane encouraged Clara to rewrite the list, including positive comments from her teachers, college supervisors and clients in Canada; her own life experiences and transferable skills from working in other jobs; and the strengths that she had already listed from facilitating or attending workshops. When the list grew to 13 points, Clara became very excited.

It was time to look at creating a goal, and Jane asked Clara to set the goal that she wanted to achieve in three months' time. She should be as precise as possible about this, deciding how many clients she wanted, what sort of clients and what percentage of the week she would spend with them. Having set the goal, she was asked to create a list of strategies that would help her achieve this. In fact, most of these had already been decided through the process of supervision. They just needed to be made more concrete. Clara's final list included the following:

- I can use my list of 13 reasons why clients want to come to me as a positive visualization. I will read it every day.

- I will increase the amount of time I spend on my business to two days a week.

- During my two days, I will rewrite my information lecture, and buy and study from a new textbook.

- I will develop my mailing list and invite people I meet at workshops to join.

- I will attend related workshops once a month in order to network with other practitioners.

- I will find a more central venue where I can hold my next information workshop, and run it once midweek and once at the weekend.

- I will make a positive achievement journal, in which I will list everything that goes well at workshops. I can print and paste the emails I have received from satisfied clients in Canada as well as those from here.

This task took Clara several days and Jane was delighted to read the email when it arrived, because it was so positive. Although Clara had implemented several strategies previously, she had been held back by her limiting beliefs about her own worth. The new list of strategies included some very practical steps such as a mailing list and finding a new workshop venue, but there was added value in the steps Clara was taking to raise her own self-esteem and feel that she was worthy of working with new clients.

Jane's final recommendation was that Clara should do a review of her strategies every two weeks. She should ask herself, 'Are my strategies working for me?' If she was not achieving any of her strategies, she should not feel guilty and blame herself. She should simply rewrite the strategy to make it more effective.

As they were now coming towards the end of the supervision, Jane asked, 'How do you feel now? Have you done enough work for this supervision or do you have further questions?' Clara wrote back to say that she was pleased with the work and would report back in three months.

This piece of supervision took place over two weeks, and covered many aspects of the supervisee's work. It began with an exploration of the current situation, and progressed towards a new goal and new strategies. Because of the slow pace, the supervisor could pick up and work with issues such as time management and self-esteem.

Different ways of working

Long-distance work opens up possibilities for supervision across cultural, ethnic and language differences. This in itself can be very exciting and stimulating for both supervisor and supervisee, because it demands an awareness and respect for diversity. Supervisors cannot take their own ethical or moral values for granted, but need to double check whether these are relevant for the supervisee. You can explore the supervisee's cultural values in order to help you come to a mutual understanding.

An internet video link is the closest to live supervision because it has face-to-face contact and concrete start and end times. It is nearly three-dimensional and can be like a phone with added value, if the service is working well. Email opens up the possibilities for a different way of working that is slower and more thoughtful, taking place over several days. The phone is useful for short sessions between face-to-face supervision sessions.

Chapter 12

Collecting and Making Resources and Props

You can approach finding your resources and props in many different ways. You can make yourself a list of materials that you want to use in your supervision sessions. Alternatively, you can allow your collection to grow organically as you find and discover new resources or props. We have noticed that when supervisees work with props there is an excitement in the room and an element of play. You can enjoy the same fun when assembling and making your own collection. Once you have gathered your resources, we suggest that you keep them together.

Toy animals and figurines

These can be bought brand new from toyshops or you can find second-hand toys in charity shops and jumble sales. They can be made of hard or soft plastic, fabric, fur, metal or other materials, and having a variety of these can extend the creative possibilities. Try to collect a range of at least 20 different toys to start with. Consider the scale of the objects that you collect. Sometimes an item that is out of scale with the rest of your collection can take on an interesting significance.

Bricks

Bricks can be any proprietary brand of wooden or plastic blocks. You can also make your own from polystyrene cut to shape and painted with acrylic colours.

Stones, shells or buttons

Collections of stones or shells can be found in DIY superstores, in garden nurseries, on the beach or by a river. To add colour and interest you can include some polished gemstones, which can be bought in bead shops or tourist shops at seaside resorts.

You can make up a collection of buttons from old family button boxes or find them in charity shops. You could also make your own out of polymer clay.

Objets trouvés

These can be collected from around the house or office. They can include, for example, seashells, coloured plastic bottle tops, pine cones, clothes pegs, corks, paper clips, old coins, cotton reels, marbles, key rings, colourful erasers, pencil sharpeners, pen tops, Christmas decorations and souvenirs.

You can also make your own objects out of bits and pieces that you find around the place. For example, you can decorate a cork, a lid or a small block of wood with paint, glitter or glued-on pieces of fabric. Caroline made a drum-like rattle by gluing two empty metal tea lights together, filled with lentils and covered with fabric. You can make interesting shapes and objects out of polymer clay. These can be any colour, cut out using pastry cutters or a craft knife and then oven baked.

Puppets

Soft toys can be used as puppets, or children's puppets can be bought from toyshops or charity shops. Here is a pattern for an oven glove-like puppet. These can be decorated with lace, buttons, felt, beads, fabric paints, sequins or feathers. You can add a tongue inside the mouth (see Figure 12.1).

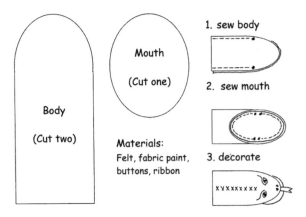

Figure 12.1 Make your own glove puppets

Stationery and art materials

The most often used resources are a big pack of white and coloured paper. You will also need a good choice of felt-tipped pens, which are all in working order. Big sheets of paper from a flipchart can also be useful as well as a pile of old magazines and newspapers, and scissors.

Keep a supply of Blu-Tack® to hand because it can be invaluable for fastening paper and other items on the wall for group members and workshop participants to view. It can also be used to fix objets trouvés or animals into a constellation.

Money

Play money can be bought at toyshops as well as through shops selling fake money for gambling games. You can spice this up by adding leftover foreign paper money.

Picture postcards

You can create a large collection of photographs of people. These can be picture postcards from charity shops, museums, art galleries and holiday destinations. Photos can also be cut out of magazines and glued on to A4 or A5 index cards. Ensure that you have a wide range of different characters and moods. Here are some examples of the diversity that you might consider: a glamorous model, a priest, a star from a black and white film, an oil painting of a duke, a child with a lollypop, a girl running with a dog, a family cuddling up by the fireside, an old man clutching some money, a pretty girl playing tennis, teenagers in front of a computer, a scientist with a microscope, a surgeon in green scrubs, a person in a wheelchair, a laughing child and a woman climbing a mountain. Make sure that you choose a wide range of pictures showing diversity in age, culture, sexual orientation, profession, religion, class and ethnicity. You will need between 20 and 100 cards.

Values cards

You can buy these as Angel cards in esoteric shops, or you can create your own using blank business cards. You can use coloured ones or a mixture of coloured and white. Each card should have a value written on it – for example, appreciation, balance, calmness, commitment, compassion, co-operation, energy, enthusiasm, flexibility, honesty, humour, integrity, listening, mindfulness, practicality, tolerance, trust or wisdom. You can also make up your own values according to the setting in which you work.

Explore and share your ideas

This is by no means a definitive list of props. We are offering it to you as a starting point for your own creativity and that of your supervisees. We would be delighted to hear what ideas you have come up with for using in creative supervision; please contact us through Jessica Kingsley Publishers.

References

Aesop (n.d.) *The Fox and the Crow.* Available at www.aesops-fables.org.uk/aesop-fable-the-fox-and-the-crow.htm, accessed on 28 August 2010.

Borton, T. (1970) *Reach, Touch and Teach.* London: Hutchinson.

Carroll, L. (1865) *Alice's Adventures in Wonderland.* London: Macmillan.

Caspari, E. and Robbins, K. (2003) *Animal Life in Nature, Myth and Dreams.* Illinois: Chiron.

Cooper, J. (1978) *An Illustrated Encyclopaedia of Traditional Symbols.* London: Thames & Hudson.

Doidge, N. (2008) *The Brain That Changes Itself.* London: Penguin.

Driscoll, J. (2000) *Practising Clinical Supervision: A Reflective Approach.* London: Bailliere Tindall.

Garro, L. and Mattingly, C. (eds) (2000) *Narrative and the Cultural Construction of Illness and Healing.* Berkeley, CA: University of California Press.

Gawain, S. (1978) *Creative Visualisation.* California: New World Library.

Hawkins, P. and Shohet, R. (1989) *Supervision in the Helping Professions: An Individual, Group and Organizational Approach.* Milton Keynes: Open University Press.

Heron, J. (1990) *Helping the Client: A Creative Practical Guide.* London: Sage Publications.

Jasper, M. (2003) *Beginning Reflective Practice.* Cheltenham: Nelson Thornes.

Johns, C. (2004) *Becoming a Reflective Practitioner.* Oxford: Blackwell.

Karpman, S. (1968) 'Fairy Tales and Script Drama Analysis.' *Transactional Analysis Bulletin 7,* 26, 39–43.

Knowles, M. (1973) *The Adult Learner: A Neglected Species.* Houston, TX: Gulf Publishing.

Lahad, M. (2000) *Creative Supervision: The Use of Expressive Arts Methods in Supervision and Self-supervision.* London: Jessica Kingsley Publishers.

Landy, R. (2003) 'Drama Therapy with Adults.' In C. Schaefer (ed.) *Play Therapy with Adults.* Hoboken, NJ: John Wiley & Sons.

Launer, J. (2002) *Narrative-based Primary Care: A Practical Guide.* Oxford: Radcliffe Medical Press.

Losier, M. (2007) *Law of Attraction.* London: Hodder & Stoughton.

Luft, J. (1984) *Group Processes: An Introduction to Group Dynamics,* 2nd edition. Mountain View, CA: Mayfield Publishing.

Minton, D. (1997) *Teaching Skills in Further and Adult Education.* London: City & Guilds/Thompson.

Moon, J. (2004) *A Handbook of Reflective and Experiential Learning. Theory and Practice.* London and New York: Routledge Falmer.

Potter, B. (1908) *The Tale of Jemima Puddleduck.* London: Frederick Warne and Co.

Proctor, B. (2000) *Group Supervision: A Guide to Creative Practice.* London: Sage Publications.

Ryan, S. (2004) *Vital Practice.* Kingscliff, NSW: Sea Change.

Satir, V. (1988) *The New Peoplemaking.* Mountain View, CA: Science and Behavior Books Inc.

Schuck, C. and Wood, J. (2007) 'Playing Reflection and Reality.' *Journal of Holistic Health Care 4,* 2, 23–27.

Silverstone, L. (2009) *Art Therapy Exercises: Inspirational and Practical Ideas to Stimulate the Imagination.* London: Jessica Kingsley Publishers.

Wosket, V. (1999) *The Therapeutic Use of Self: Counselling Practice, Research and Supervision.* London: Brunner/Routledge.

Zeldin, T. (1998) *Conversation: How Talk Can Change Your Life.* London: Harvill Press.

Further Reading

Bolton, G. (2010) *Reflective Practice: Writing and Professional Development*. London: Sage Publications.

Buzan, T. (1977) *Make the Most of Your Mind*. London: Pan Books.

Buzan, T. (1989) *Use Your Head*. London: BBC Active.

Cameron, J. (1995) *The Artist's Way: A Course in Discovering and Recovering your Creative Self*. London: Pan Books.

Cameron, J. (2002) *Walking in This World: Practical Strategies for Creativity*. London: Rider.

Cantore, S., Lewis, S. and Passmore, J. (2008) *Appreciative Inquiry for Change Management using AI to Facilitate Organizational Development*. London: Kogan Page.

Carroll, M. (1996) *Counselling Supervision: Theory Skills and Practice*. London: Cassell.

Carroll, M. and Gilbert, M. (2005) *On Being A Supervisee: Creating Learning Partnerships*. London: Vukani Publishing.

Draper, R., Gower, M. and Huffington, C. (1990) *Teaching Family Therapy*. London: Karnac Books.

Edwards, B. (1988) *Drawing on the Right Side of the Brain: How to Unlock Your Artistic Talent*. Glasgow: Fontana/Collins.

Greenhalgh, T. and Hurwitz, B. (eds) (1998) *Narrative Based Medicine*. London: BMJ Books.

Hellinger, B. (2003) *Farewell Family Constellations with Descendants of Victims and Perpetrators*. Heidelberg: Carl-Auer-Systeme Verlag.

Heron, J. (2008) *Helping the Client. A Creative Guide*, 5th edition. London: Sage Publications.

Heron, J. (2009) *The Complete Facilitator's Handbook*. London: Kogan Page.

Hunt, C. and Sampson, F. (eds) *The Self on the Page: Theory and Practice of Creative Writing in Personal Development*. London: Jessica Kingsley Publishers.

Jasper, M. (2003) *Beginning Reflective Practice*. Cheltenham: Nelson Thornes.

Keleman, S. (1979) *Somatic Reality*. Berkeley, CA: Center Press.

King, T. (2003) *The Truth About Stories*. Minneapolis: University of Minnesota Press.

Lipton, B. (2009) *The Biology of Belief*. California: Hay House.

Page, S. and Wosket, V. (2001) *Supervising the Counsellor: A Cyclical Model*. Hove: Routledge.

Pearson, C. (1991) *Awakening the Heroes Within. Twelve Archetypes to Help Us Find Ourselves and Transform Our World*. San Francisco, CA: HarperCollins.

Pease, A. (1997) *Body Language: How to Read Others' Thoughts by their Gestures*. London: Sheldon Press.

Pease, A. and Pease, B. (2004) *The Definitive Book of Body Language*. London: Orion Books.

Schaefer, C. (ed.) (2003) *Play Therapy with Adults*. New Jersey: John Wiley & Sons.

Selvini, M.P., Boscolo, L., Cecchin, G. and Prata, G. (1980) 'Hypothesizing – Circularity – Neutrality: Three Guidelines for the Conductor of the Session', *Family Process 19*, 1, 3–12.

Shipton, G. (ed.) (2000) *Supervision of Psychotherapy and Counselling: Making a Place to Think*. Milton Keynes: Open University Press.

Tomm, K. (1988) 'Interventive Interviewing: Part 111. Intending to Ask Linear, Circular, Strategic, or Reflexive Questions?' *Family Process 27*, 1, 1–15.

Yalom, I. (1985) *The Theory and Practice of Group Psychotherapy*. New York: Basic Books.

Index